'Martin Knight has produced a marvellously detailed chronicle of social history, based on the family reminiscences of 100-year-old Nell, the Battersea Girl, whose thorn-sharp memory reaches into the past with such telling effect. The cumulative power of the narrative is a remarkable achievement and such a book – about people so ordinary as to be extraordinary – will be enjoyed by whoever picks it up.'

– Alan Sillitoe, author of *Saturday Night and Sunday Morning* and *The Loneliness of the Long Distance Runner*

'A vivid account of a London working-class family in the early twentieth century when the south bank of the Thames was the children's playground; everybody knew everybody and life was as dramatic as a Shakespeare play. This is living oral history as witnessed by Nell, the author's grandmother, and is absolutely fascinating. By the end of the book, I knew Nell so well, and I admired and loved her. I also knew what it was like to be a working-class woman before feminism had kicked in.'

– Nell Dunn, author of *Up the Junction* and *Poor Cow*

Martin Knight is the author of the novel *Common People*. He has also co-authored books with Peter Osgood, George Best and Dave Mackay. He lives in London and Norfolk with his wife and children.

Battersea Girl

Battersea Girl

Tracing a London Life

Martin Knight

MAINSTREAM
PUBLISHING
EDINBURGH AND LONDON

First published in Great Britain in 2006 by
MAINSTREAM PUBLISHING COMPANY (EDINBURGH) LTD
7 Albany Street
Edinburgh EH1 3UG

ISBN 1 84596 150 1

A catalogue record for this book is available from the British Library

Typeset in Garamond and Lucida

Printed and bound in Great Britain by
William Clowes Ltd, Beccles, Suffolk

To Ellen Tregent (1888–1988)
Who else?

and my dad, Harry Knight,
who lit up the past and my life

Contents

Introduction

In 1973, when I was 15 years of age, I elected to take three Certificates of Secondary Education (CSE) as the culmination of my comprehensive schooling. In the hierarchy of school-leaving examinations of the time these were the bottom rungs of the academic ladder, behind the O level and the A level. Their purpose was, perhaps, to give some focus to boys and girls who lacked academic ambition and application but showed signs of having absorbed some of the teachings of their previous five years. The three subjects I chose were the only ones I enjoyed and in which I paid any attention: English, history and art. It was no coincidence that the teachers of these subjects at my school all treated their pupils as human beings and had the skills and enthusiasm to make the lessons interesting. Most of the teaching staff I had come across up to then were either counting time to 3.30 p.m., the six-week-long summer holiday or their eventual early retirement.

The history mistress, Miss Benthall, a young lady fresh from teacher-training college, suggested I base my final examination project on my family history. She obviously believed there would be more chance of my seeing this through than a study of the Napoleonic wars or medieval crop-rotation systems. I was aware of parts of my ancestry through my parents, but most importantly my paternal grandmother was still alive and living in Battersea, aged 85. She knew it all. She'd been telling us for years but nobody had been listening.

Grandma lived alone in a council flat at the top of Lavender Hill and fortnightly, on a Saturday, I accompanied my dad to visit her. As a young boy, it was exciting. The train journey up to Clapham Junction, then entering the mythical land of London; the red buses, black taxis and busy markets; the general hubbub unfamiliar then in semi-rural Epsom where I lived; the climb up the hill; and the last-second visit to the off-licence to buy her a large brown bottle of Guinness.

On entering her flat, I was immediately immersed in a dark, dank world. The curtains were nearly always drawn (my grandmother was so contrary she probably opened them at night) and a musty smell of old empty biscuit tins prevailed. Besides a tiny kitchenette and an even tinier bathroom, the flat consisted of one room dominated by her large imperious double bed with Jesus Christ looking serenely down at the pillows from a crucifix on the wall above them. At the foot of the bed stood a small table, covered in a leathery tablecloth, with a chair at each end. On the table lay Grandma's magnifying glass and the *Daily Express*. Her habit of reading through the glass was a cause of great amusement to us children. In the corner was a television that already seemed ancient, sporting a preposterous aerial, like an upturned tuning fork, which dwarfed the actual set. Compared to our home, which itself was only a three-bedroom council house, her living accommodation seemed like a cupboard. Sometimes she tried to persuade us to accept a piece of Christmas cake or a ham sandwich, but Dad normally said we had just eaten. 'The problem is,' he would advise later, 'there's no telling exactly which Christmas the cake dates from.'

On one visit, Dad explained to her that I was producing a family history for my schoolwork and asked if she could help by putting flesh on some old bones, starting as far back as she knew. In a flash, she transported us back in time by 150 years, producing a prayer book from her bedside drawer that had belonged to her grandfather and had his pencilled inscription on the inside cover.

'It says *Patrick* Bradshaw. I thought his name was James,' queried Dad.

Grandma then told us both how my great-great-grandfather had come over to England from Ireland when the potato famine of the late 1840s struck, thereby interrupting a centuries-old pattern of agricultural living, and that he had changed his name to combat prejudice against Irish immigrants. In a single sentence, she had tied the family into the general history of the country and beyond.

So began an unfolding of the family ancestry. As we led her down particular roads on numerous subsequent visits, her story became ever more fascinating and convoluted. Her recall was vivid and precise. We heard of men making a living on the Thames, a river that had claimed the lives of at least two close family members, the discovery of a drowned aristocrat's body and the curse of the ensuing reward. She talked of labour strikes and family feuds, of suicides and fatal accidents, poverty and depression, of the spectre of drink, murder and wars, and of the bombardment of Battersea by the Luftwaffe. But she also spoke of the love, the loyalty and the laughs, of weddings, babies and trips to the Kent hop fields, all of which made life bearable. Indeed, she was never maudlin or sad as she recalled these often harrowing passages of her life. That was life. That was how it was. Everyone she knew was in the same boat. Although she took great pride in the strides made by her descendants and recognised the growing comfort of the modern world, it was a boat she would have happily climbed back into if she could.

There was so much information to go on, but Dad warned that we should not take everything she told us for granted. Much of what she had revealed was new even to him and he was sceptical. When she made an aside that she attended the great cricketer W.G. Grace's funeral because she was, for a time, his charlady, Dad interrupted. 'Are you sure, Mum? I haven't heard that before.'

'Course I'm sure. You couldn't mistake 'im, could yer? Not with that bleedin' long beard.'

We visited Somerset House in London and collected what birth, marriage and death certificates we could and these in turn would prompt new questions. Sometimes Grandma may have had a small detail wrong, but generally everything we found backed up what she was telling us. We visited the newspaper archives at the Lavender Hill library, almost next door to my grandmother's flat, and confirmed many of the other events she had described.

In a very short period, she gave me enough material for my project. I focused mainly on family events that tied in with historical ones and submitted the thing. It was all blue ink and felt pens interspersed with glued-in copies of birth, marriage and death certificates. Pride of place went to a copy of a letter sent to my grandmother from Winston Churchill, at the time Secretary of State for War, commiserating with her on the loss of her husband in the Great War. Miss Benthall praised the finished product highly and was amazed at the amount of research she thought had gone into it. I did not let on that nearly all the information had come from my grandmother's lips and bedside drawers.

When I was eventually awarded a Grade 2 CSE rather than the Grade 1, as Miss Benthall had expected, she said it must have been because of a poor performance in the written examination. She was right there – I never sat it. My interest had moved on. Whilst I continued to visit my grandmother until her death at 100 years of age in 1988, I never really dug much further on the family history front, although I continued to absorb the stories she told me. Events of 70 years earlier were recounted as if they happened yesterday: what she said to him and what he said to her, who was a rum one and who wasn't. Sitting at that table and listening, by now sharing the Guinness as an adult, I was as close as I could get to travelling back in time without a Tardis of my very own.

In the last couple of years, my interest in genealogy has been reawakened, mainly by the Genes Reunited website, part of the Friends Reunited stable. Within a few weeks of uploading our family tree as I knew it, I was contacted by two separate members who had registered at the site and who shared the same great-great-grandfather in Battersea. Dots were quickly joined and even more of my grandmother's apparent musings were confirmed. It led to the discovery of two living relatives – a niece and a nephew of Grandma – both now in their 80s and both still living in Battersea. They told me so much about my grandmother's middle years. It was a delight to find them because not only did they share Grandma's facial features but they also spoke with the distinctive old Battersea accent I thought I would never hear again and which I had often tried to conjure up in my mind. If Genes Reunited continues to grow at its current rate, within a few years everyone really will be connected if they so wish.

From Genes Reunited, I moved on to the 1901 Census site and

then on to earlier census information from various other portals. My searches took me to war graves, the records of the Company of Watermen and Lightermen, newspaper archives, police records, war diaries and much, much more – all this practically without leaving my desk.

Slowly but surely a picture emerged of my family history with detail I could never have imagined. More importantly, I could put my grandmother's eventful life into context, something that had not been easy 30 years earlier. Belatedly, I began to appreciate (as much as one can who does not live it) her life and her times. I regretted laughing at her quaintness, her quirkiness, her superstitions and antiquated ideas. I realised what a remarkable woman she was and decided the least I could do was write a book about her life.

As she would say, you couldn't make it up.

Therefore *Battersea Girl* is a novel of sorts, but it is chiefly a story of my grandmother's long life. I have borrowed from the library of poetic licence and inserted a couple of fictional themes and characters and merged one or two others. I have mixed up some names, places and events because, after all, I am not the only person descended from and connected to the characters in this book. And I have guessed what the various people did and said in different circumstances. I have also had to follow a number of thought processes in deciding what made certain people do certain things. Nevertheless, I would estimate that 80 per cent of the events recounted did actually happen and are supported by documentary evidence.

For me, the remarkable thing about Ellen Tregent's life is how unremarkable it was for the period. So many people I have contacted who are also researching their family histories have found similar stories and patterns. If the book prompts just a few people to mine their family's past and derive just some of the enjoyment and fulfilment that I have, then I judge it to have been a worthwhile exercise.

And Mum, don't fret, we'll do your side next.

Martin Knight
Norfolk, 2006

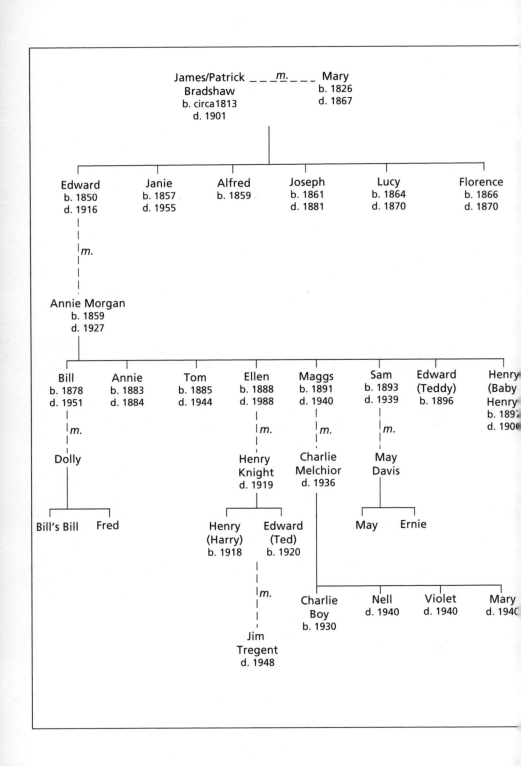

I

Birthday Girl

The old lady sat in the wheelchair and frowned at the people around her. It had been a real effort getting her out of bed and sitting upright and the disruption still irked her. The nurses had made her as comfortable as possible, propping her upright with pillows and cushions. A pretty little blonde girl of about five years of age stood beside her, as if on guard, and gently rested on her hand the old lady's, so thin it resembled a transparent glove pulled tight on a skeletal hand, and stroked it tenderly. 'You all right, Grandma?' she said softly.

A man with a large chain around his neck, who the old lady had never clapped eyes on before, stood in the middle of the room. He had a silly upturned moustache of the style once favoured by RAF fighter pilots with names like Trubshawe. With a rattling cough, he cleared his throat and began to speak loudly. 'I am honoured to be invited here today to mark the occasion of the 100th birthday of Ellen Tregent. Although I had never had the pleasure of Ellen's acquaintance until this afternoon, I am told that she has been a resident of Wandsworth for all of her 100 years and has led a full and exciting life. It is a remarkable achievement and I am sure that she and all of her family and friends here today are very proud. I would like you all to raise your glasses to Ellen. To Ellen. One hundred years young.'

'To Nell,' chorused the guests, old and young, preferring not to echo the mayor's little pun and calling the old lady by the name they all used. The small girl climbed up on the chair, placed her glass of orange to the old lady's lips and gently tipped it, but Nell's mouth remained resolutely closed. A small trickle of liquid ran down her chin.

Although, one by one, the guests came and spoke to Nell, she did not reply. She could not. She would have liked to, but she was simply unable. Her brain still worked, but the link that enabled her to communicate her thoughts had been broken months before. If she could have spoken, she'd have told the Mayor of Wandsworth to 'sling his hook' for starters. He'd never found the need to come and see her and celebrate her life for 99 years and 364 days, she would have said, so why now? As an avid consumer of television news and current affairs in the 1960s and '70s, she was reminded by the mayor's moustache of two men who sported similar ridiculous hair displays on their top lips and who filled her television screens almost daily for a period. One was a Post Office trade-union leader, the other a Tory MP. Nell thought them both fools and show-offs, and felt this man must be the same. In her part of the world flamboyancy of any kind was the eighth deadly sin.

Nell knew most of the people in the room but couldn't name them, especially the great-grandchildren. There were so many of them and they were nearly all blonde – a Bradshaw trait, in childhood at least. But she knew that the little girl holding her hand was Michelle, her eldest great-granddaughter. Although they were separated by 95 years, they enjoyed a special bond. Neither could describe it, but that tie was nature's way of connecting the past to the future. Michelle was kind and sweet, and preferred to fuss over the older members of the family than charge around the room chasing balloons excitedly with the other children.

In the corner, sitting alone sipping a cup of tea, was Mrs Bruno, a large black woman of some 50 years. She had been Nell's district nurse for the last decade, right up until she had finally entered the nursing home. She was sitting upright and had not yet removed her large overcoat. Nell wanted to smile at her, call out and make her feel more at home.

She remembered the first time Mrs Bruno had appeared at the door. As she had loomed in the doorway, her large frame and colour had scared Nell. She had told her to clear off, that she didn't want her sort in her house and would complain to the council. Fortunately Mrs Bruno was by then accustomed to such welcomes from the very old residents of Battersea, and swept the remarks aside and set about making Nell a pot of tea. It took a year or so but the two women developed a real fondness and respect for one another, and Mrs Bruno became the last new friend that Nell made.

A smiling, kindly grey-haired man came over and sat down beside Nell. He tugged up his trousers as he settled into his seat. It was a family habit that had been unwittingly passed down the generations. Little Michelle beamed at her granddad as he unfolded a piece of paper. 'This is a telegram from the Queen, Mum, wishing you a happy 100th birthday. How about that, eh?'

'And she says you can have tea with her if you make 200,' chimed in another voice from behind her chair. Its owner was more portly than the other man, but there was no doubting they were brothers. These were Nell's boys – Harry and Ted. *Good boys*, she thought as she listened to them. *Never a spot of bother.* Both had left Battersea almost as soon as they could shave and had done well, living lives of comfort and prosperity that Nell could never have envisaged. But they'd always bring their families up to Battersea to see her when they could and she went to them alternately every Christmas. Standing beside Ted, smiling at Nell, was Charlie Boy, a cousin of the Knight brothers. Charlie was no boy, knocking on for 60 years now. He had particular reason to be here, saluting Nell today. A couple of the young children could not take their eyes off him, as they studied the patchwork of different shades and contours of skin on one side of his face and the sudden jerking of his body that was so violent they thought his head might roll off. *Don't stare, it's rude.*

Nell tried to smile and acknowledge her boys, but instead she looked straight ahead with knitted brow. She was extraordinarily content, though, here in the bosom of her family. The struggle was over. The spectre of war and strife seemed to have slunk away. Harry and Ted had managed to find work all of their lives: one had been employed in an office and the other owned his own business – something to which people from Nell's generation and Battersea very rarely aspired. They now lived in comfortable retirement, running cars and enjoying foreign holidays. Her grandchildren were also all in work now, doing jobs with titles that she did not recognise or understand: accountants and consultants, software engineers and personnel managers. They enjoyed a lifestyle and level of mobility Nell could not relate to. When they visited their grandmother they spoke about the limited common ground they had, namely their parents – Nell's children – and the past. She could talk for hours about the past. She had so much of it. She was a great one for peppering oaths of despair in her everyday conversation – Lord 'elp us! What is the world coming to? Gawd forbid – but when she looked at her family and their lives, even she conceded that the world was surely a far better place overall than the one she was born into. It had to be.

The party did not last more than a couple of hours on this cold March afternoon. Weightless flakes of snow fell and disintegrated on the lawn outside the window. The Mayor of Wandsworth left as soon as it was politely possible. The uniformed chauffeur held open the door of the 22-year-old Rolls-Royce and the mayor stepped in and travelled back to his semi-detached house on the Wimbledon border. Later in the evening, he'd be climbing into his six-year-old Ford Escort and driving to Sainsbury's for the weekly shop with his wife. The photographer from the *Wandsworth Borough News* followed the mayor's lead and this was the signal for others to stand up, brush down their trousers and pick up keys. It was a party in name only. The guests knew they were attending a celebration, but the mood was tempered by the unspoken realisation that for most of them it would be the last time they would see Nell Tregent.

The helpers at the nursing home started to make themselves visible and markedly asked Nell a couple of times if she was tired. They, more than most, knew they would get no answer. Mrs Redcliffe, who ran the nursing home, came over to chat to Harry and Ted. 'She's a strong woman, your mother.'

'She is that,' said Harry.

'I bet she's seen a few changes in her lifetime.'

'She has, for sure,' he nodded again.

'What did she do for a living?'

'Survived,' Ted returned, slightly irked by the emptiness of the question. What did she think his mother did – ran ICI?

Everyone kissed Nell goodbye, planting lips on her forehead as they filed out of the dining-room area. Most were heading out to the suburbs and beyond, where their routines would be quickly resumed. There were groceries to buy, homework to be done, wine to be drunk and arguments to be had.

Little Michelle had still not let go of Nell's hand and when any of the toddlers came near for their kiss goodbye, she shielded Nell's slight and delicate frame. Finally, as the last of the guests left the room, Michelle climbed up again on Nell's chair and whispered into her ear, 'I've got to go now, Grandma. Mummy and Daddy are in the car. I love you.'

Nell slowly and with great effort lifted a trembling hand and stroked the little girl's cheek with the side of her finger. 'Bye, bye, sweetheart.'

'Bye, bye, Grandma.'

Michelle ran out into the drive, spraying gravel in her haste, 'Mummy! Daddy! Grandma just spoke to me. She just said goodbye to me. She did. She really did.'

'OK, darling, come on now, hop in. We've got to get off,' said her father, who had timed his exit perfectly to narrowly avoid the worst of the Wandsworth one-way-system rush-hour traffic jams and to arrive home in time to at least mow the front lawn before it became too dark.

* * *

Nell had lost count of the years. She remembers 1980. Her Ted was 60 years old in that year and she'd been well enough to go to his party down in Sussex. Ted's wife, Eileen, had collected her in the car and dropped her back again at 10 p.m. And she remembers Prince Charles and Lady Diana getting married and all the fuss surrounding it, but she could not say definitely if that was before or after Ted's 60th. She'd continued to visit Harry and Ted after 1980, but her memories became blurred and the Christmases merged into one. Before 1980, there was no confusion whatsoever. Years and dates were Nell's thing. Always had been. From a very young age, she had assumed the responsibility of family archivist, mainly because nobody else wanted to do it (or could do it as well as her). She knew all the birthdays, where people lived, and when and who was buried where. Whether she was your mother, sister, aunt, cousin or grandmother, Nell's birthday card was the third certainty in life. Even after a person had left this world, she continued to acknowledge their birthdays. When her sons had visited, Nell often started the conversation with something along the lines of, 'Uncle John, your grandfarver's bruvver, would 'ave been 128 on Thursday.'

Back in her flat, there were photographs, familiar ornaments and artefacts to ground her. There was the prayer book that had belonged to her grandfather, with the occasional passage that must have had some special meaning to James Bradshaw all those years ago underlined in pencil, and the flowers, now 150 years old, pressed flat into its pages. The photograph of her niece dressed in a black cloak, wearing a mortar-board, at her graduation ceremony. It was a first for a member of the extended family to go to university and therefore Nell found it easy to remember that year, 1962. Everyone was so proud of Helen. Before her, the only time the Bradshaws had come into contact with anyone from a university was when, as children, they hurried down to Putney Bridge to watch the start of the Oxford–Cambridge boat race.

On the mantelpiece, next to the Double Diamond ashtray, which had somehow found its way to Nell's flat from the Cornet and Horse pub, was a china model of a horse in flight. A scroll on the base revealed its name: Arkle. Harry had bought this for his mother in 1966 after the horse won the Cheltenham Gold Cup for the third time. Nell liked a bet and had latched on to Arkle very early in his career and, she claimed, had won hundreds of pounds on him over his racing life. The boys doubted this, as any stake money would have had to come from her paltry pension, but with Mum they could never be sure.

In the drawer next to the bed was a tin of face cream with a tiny illustration on the cap of a Victorian man and lady courting. The lady holds a parasol and the man is bowing towards her, Walter Raleigh-style, the manufacturer's implication being that if you purchased this face cream you were more likely to be pursued by an eligible and handsome young bachelor. Nell remembers buying it in a small shop in Hastings and the year was most certainly 1919. She had gone there for the day on a special train from Clapham Junction packed with Battersea and Clapham day-trippers. Her husband, Henry, had not long returned from a final stint in France clearing the debris of the First World War and was very weak from being gassed earlier on in the conflict. He was also suffering from a selection of other war-related ailments.

A few weeks previously, he had arrived in Battersea to discover that his wife was hopping down in Kent. Keen to surprise her, he made his way down into the Kent countryside on shanks's pony and located Nell among the vines. She welcomed the wretched man with, 'What the 'ell are you doing 'ere?' followed by, 'You look 'alf dead.' Which, she often mused later, he was.

Poor Henry came on the train that summer's day in 1919, though, despite his collapsing health, and they left baby Harry with Nell's mother, Annie. Like nearly all of the young men packing into the carriages, his suit was now ill fitting and his cap comically almost slid down over his eyes. The war had rendered him almost skeletal – there had been hardly an ounce of fat on him before he enlisted five long years earlier. Most poignant for Nell on his return was that he now carried his wedding ring in his waistcoat pocket because his fingers had become so thin it would no longer stay on. Large brown bottles of stout, pale ale and Guinness were being passed up and down the carriages and although Nell managed to knock two or three back on the journey out, Henry had barely sipped his.

There was a general air of excitement and chatter as the train steamed out of London. Couples picked up their relationships, young women coyly surveyed the returning menfolk, looking for husbands, and single men savoured the peace, contemplating the revived prospect of their lifetime unfolding.

After disgorging at the railway station, the now boisterous crowd headed straight for the seafront, not giving a second glance to the old crumbling castle perched doggedly on the top of the West Hill. They were not here on a history field trip, after all. Nell and Henry walked along the promenade with all the others, feeling the fresh sea wind whipping their faces and hearing the cackle of Londoners at play on the beach beside them. At the pier, they turned around and walked back down the front, leaving the Battersea mob to pass through the turnstiles: they took the pretty little lift, like a train carriage, up to the top of the East Hill, preferring the solitude of the countryside to the bustle of the pier and the tinkling of the penny arcades. They walked arm in arm up and down the undulating hills towards Fairlight Glen, keeping the sea to their right and drinking in the novelty of being alone together. They did not pass a single soul. Even out on the ocean there were no solitary ships of any kind. Nell and Henry felt like the only two people in England. They sat on the so-called Lover's Seat, where, local legend had it, a lady, who lost her young man at sea, sat at night and flashed a torch forlornly in the hope that one day he would return to shore.

Before they reached the village of Pett Level, and realising they would have to turn back if they were not to be in danger of missing the train home, they laid out their coats in a secluded area and made love. Nell remembers the year and the occasion so well because she and Henry only made love twice. In later life and in private conversation with the female members of her family, she professed to be immensely proud of this fact; as if the physical abstinence was evidence of strength of character and a demonstration that sex was for procreation and nothing else. Harry was the result of their first time, when Henry was home on leave in 1917 and they had married hastily, and Ted would be the upshot of this union in Hastings. Ted was born in early 1920 and by that time Henry, his father, had been dead for six months.

Back at the nursing home, there were no such ornaments and artefacts to help Nell reassemble and order her memories. She had no idea what year it was. She didn't even know the day or hour. She vaguely understood she'd reached a milestone that day and that people were gathered to see her. She heard people say she was 100 but couldn't be sure exactly what that meant, although she realised it seemed to be important to everyone. Her day was regulated by the agenda of the home. She was woken, washed and fed. For small periods of the day she was put into a chair and then put back to bed. Sometimes, she was wheeled into the TV room, but she wished she wasn't. She couldn't focus on the picture and the dialogue did not reach her ears. Nell slept all the time, or at least that is how it appeared because her eyes were normally closed. Behind her lids, though, she was replaying her life in her mind and the further back she travelled, the more vivid the detail. There was more than enough there, in her head, to keep her occupied and to pass her final days.

II

Oh, What Has
Old Ireland Done?

Give me three grains of corn, Mother,
Only three grains of corn.
'Twill keep what little life I have
Till the coming of the morn.
For I'm dying of hunger and cold, Mother,
Dying of hunger and cold,
And the agony of such a death
My lips have never told.
Oh, what has old Ireland done, Mother,
Oh, what has old Ireland done,
That the world looks on and sees them starve,
Perishing one by one?
There is many a brave heart, Mother,
That is dying of hunger and cold,
While only across the channel, Mother,

Thousands are rolling their gold.
Oh, how can I look to you, Mother,
Oh, how can I look to you
For bread to feed your starving child
When you are starving too?
I dreamed of bread in my sleep, Mother,
The sight was heaven to see!
I awoke with an eager and famishing lip
And you had no bread for me.

If she could have spoken, Nell would still have been able to recite the words now. Grandpa Bradshaw would sit her on his lap when she was a small girl and tell her tales of Ireland and what a wonderful, beautiful land it was. He'd sing her songs and recite poems, such as 'Give Me Three Grains of Corn, Mother', until she went to her bed with the romantic images of the Emerald Isle dancing in her head. When she was a little older and Grandpa was in the final years of his life, he explained to her about the terrible famine and what the poem was really about. That between 1841 and 1851, Ireland's population of eight million dwindled to six million, and of those lost in just a decade, half had died and the other half had emigrated. Her grandfather spoke of the Irish people who starved when the potatoes went bad and how he and many others dragged their emaciated bodies and crushed spirits aboard the coffin boats bound for Britain and America. They were called coffin boats because by the time those destined for America arrived in port at least a third of the passengers had been slung overboard on the journey when there was no breath left in their bodies. He told the young girl how once, back in his home town of Galway, a desperate and starving man had found a body washed up in the bay and removed the heart, liver and kidneys to take home for his family to eat. 'These were good people, Nell, good people,' he'd sigh painfully, shaking his head at the memory. A film of tears would then form over his eyes as he inhaled deeply on his long, white clay pipe.

Nell didn't know her grandfather's name was Patrick until after he died and she saw the inscription inside the Bible he had left her. Also, on his baptism certificate he was Patrick, but on his death certificate he was James. As the custodian of the family's sparse documentation, Nell noticed these things. Her father had explained to her that not only did James Bradshaw have to flee Ireland or face dying of starvation and disease in the 1840s, he then also encountered cruel prejudice once in England and had had to drop his Christian name to even have a chance of finding suitable work. He gave himself the name James: a safe bet, he thought, as it had been the name of more than one English king. His real surname was possibly Brady or Bradshaugh (unlike Britain in the mid-nineteenth century, written records of names and events in Ireland were very limited, and the spelling of names would depend wholly on the person transcribing them) and somewhere along the line this had been anglicised to Bradshaw – although at the time James could not write his name. It is likely that whenever his name was recorded, 'Bradshaw' is how an Englishman decided to spell it. James would not have known to correct it.

The English did not welcome the influx of Irish from over the water, calling them 'bogtrotters', among other things. They looked upon the Irish as savages and criminals with limited intelligence. If James heard the jibe once that the potato famine was caused by the Irish people forgetting where they had planted their potatoes, he heard it a thousand times. Over the years, in an effort to survive amid such racism, James also had to work hard to disguise his accent – something he resented more than anything else. Only in his last years, when he would openly pine for his homeland, did he allow his natural Irish lilt to return to his speech. He had left parents, who he was sure must have died soon after his departure, and his four older siblings, two sisters and two brothers. The brothers had become priests and the sisters nuns, he heard. James explained that the family was no more pious than the next one, but the prospect of guaranteed warmth, food and shelter would have been too tempting for them. Nell felt his pain at not really knowing the fate of his family and his having no real means of ever finding out. The old man enchanted her and she decided that before she died she would visit Galway Bay and that if she ever had children, she'd give old Patrick his name back.

* * *

James (Patrick) Bradshaw, aged 34, and his younger wife, Mary, arrived in England in 1847. They had left no children behind, although three had died at birth or in infancy before the famine had rendered the land barren, and the cholera and disease had set in. They disembarked at Liverpool, along with hundreds of others, and found the city awash with their fellow countrymen and women, sleeping in the streets and tramping around aimlessly. Disease and despair hung in the air. Many would never move further than a few miles from the point where they first stepped onto English soil. James and Mary had just enough money to get them to London, the only other English city they had heard of and where, they were told, they stood more chance of finding work, food and shelter. James told Nell of their wonder when they saw their first locomotive train steam past them on the journey: they did not even know what a train was. A fellow passenger, who joined the coach at Leicester, advised them to head for the Kennington, Lambeth and Battersea areas of London, where, he said, work could be found building the new railways and terminuses.

Oh, What Has Old Ireland Done?

The couple found shelter during their first days and nights in the busy city in a Catholic church hall in Kennington. They were comforted to find that many of their people were already there and, although conditions were cramped and deprived, they were living and eating. On only his third day in London, James found work. He was hired to lay railway track from Nine Elms to the grand new station opening up the River Thames to be named Waterloo, after the great British military victory that was still very much in living memory. He was never to experience a day's unemployment again whilst he was able-bodied and he was immensely proud of that fact. James and Mary found lodgings in a house off South Lambeth Road, originally built to accommodate one household but now filled with four or more families, with a mother and three children even living in the cellar. But it was welcome to them and they began to put down roots. They were not lonely, as Irish immigrants were still arriving thick and fast, and a community within a community was quickly forming.

When the railway construction was complete, the gang James had worked with were moving on and he had the opportunity of a couple more years' work on the Leeds and Thirsk Railway, but he did not wish to uproot again so looked around for alternative employment. He found this eventually in the timber yards by the river in Battersea and started a family connection with the Thames that would survive for well over a century. The river would give him and his descendants life and sustenance, but it would also take it away.

James began work as a sawyer, literally sawing up huge felled trees brought down the river on barges into lengths of wood. These were then loaded up on more barges for use in the construction industry. It was backbreaking toil and, like many of the river workers, they were paid at three-monthly intervals. The wages would arrive by river on heavily guarded boats so as to avoid highwaymen and robbers. The quarterly pay day was a cause for much celebration among the riverfolk. With his cash in his pocket, James would pay off the credit he had accumulated with his landlord, his butcher, his grocer and various other tradesmen – and only then would he adjourn to the inn and have his only very good drink of the quarter.

James and Mary Bradshaw had their first son in England in 1850. They called him Edward, another good English name with a royal pedigree. At the same time, they moved downriver to Battersea, nearer to the sawmill where James worked. Battersea was growing fast. Twenty years earlier, it had been little more than a village next to a bustling riverside industry; all around were market gardens, many growing asparagus, and up on the hill lavender was farmed and sold. But then the railways arrived. The large depot at Nine Elms was established and, in 1863, Clapham Junction, the huge rail metropolis, was constructed. Battersea rapidly became home to the rail-support industry, goods yards and locomotive manufacturing, and soon all manner of rail-associated light industry sprang up. Workers flowed into the area and row upon row of small terraced houses were hastily erected to accommodate them all. James and his family settled in one of these in Sleaford Street on the border of Battersea and Nine Elms and close to the river. They shared the house with another family, the father of which worked as a stoker in the nearby gas works. The house was built with red- and mustard-coloured bricks and was mid-terrace in a row of eight. There was a large room downstairs and one upstairs; the Bradshaws occupied the space on the ground floor. Out the back was a tiny yard where coal, a tin bath and toilet buckets were kept and that yard connected to the backyard of the house from the next road.

Although one room was small for three people – and it was destined to become much smaller as new children arrived – it was solid and neat unlike the older houses down on the river. These had been built in the previous century, mainly of wood, with no foundations, and they seemed to lean into one another and sag in the middle like a collapsed concertina. When the river was high, the water lapped around their doors and the boats belonging to the watermen bobbed in front of their windows. The families living in these houses were the real river people: they practically lived in it and were part of its flotsam and jetsam.

James was always keen to improve his lot and was never less than grateful for the salvation and opportunities that the move to England had afforded him. Whilst sensitive to the plight of his countrymen and aware of the widely held beliefs that it was the English who had visited these disasters on the Irish, he rarely passed comment. He had a life to lead and a family to feed and he would do everything in his power to achieve those aims.

Working in the timber yards, he came into regular contact with the watermen and lightermen who ploughed their trade up and down the Thames. They were the taxi and lorry drivers of their time: the watermen transporting people up, down and across the river in an age when fewer bridges spanned the Thames, while the lightermen ferried cargo from dock to dock and loaded and unloaded ships and boats. Each owned or rented the boat or barge that he navigated with long oars called sweeps, and, most appealingly to James, was his own master. They controlled their own destiny.

Trade on the river was growing before his eyes and the demand for lightermen seemed unquenchable, so James decided he would train to become one. This involved first finding a sponsor, then serving a long apprenticeship and paying an entrance fee, and then some years of subsisting on even lower wages, but he knew the move would eventually pay dividends.

Meanwhile, he practised some form of birth control, ever

conscious of the pressure on the family budget, for Edward did not have the company of a sibling until 1857, when Janie was born. By this time, James had purchased his first boat and was a full member of the Company of Watermen and Lightermen. It was a significant move up the employment ladder on the river. One of young Edward's earliest and most treasured memories was with his father down by the moorings in the afternoon sun, cleaning the new-but-old boat and getting a man to paint 'Galway Bay' on the side.

His sister Janie's earliest memory was of being taken by her mother, father and brother down to the riverside to watch The Female Blondin crossing the Thames on a tightrope. Charles Blondin, from whom this lady had taken her name, was a worldwide celebrity, having crossed Niagara Falls on a tightrope. He had also delighted Londoners with high-wire acts at Crystal Palace, among other places in the capital. Nevertheless, the crowds turned out in their thousands and waited with bated breath as the lady mounted the tightrope, which was fixed at one side to the Crucible Works and crossed to the Chelsea side of the Thames. Much to the delight of a baying crowd, she toppled into the water not halfway across and had to be plucked out of the dirty river by some laughing watermen.

Either James and Edward or James and another young apprentice would work the *Galway Bay* all the hours God sent, James operating the almost preposterously long oars skilfully, steering the barge along river and negotiating the tides deftly to reach his destination. He particularly liked going out at night when the river was still and quiet, but when boats and ships still moored at any one of the burgeoning docks and harbours all along the Thames. 'First come, first served,' he always said.

The work was highly strenuous, for not only was he working the sweeps but also loading and unloading cargo. However, he was never happier. There was no more waiting months for his wages, and he got out what he put in. He had to compete with the stevedores on the ground and other lightermen for his work, but he always managed to make a living. The river was an artery of industry, with more ships and more goods arriving into the capital every year. During the day, it could sometimes take hours to get from Battersea up to the huge docks in the east of London such was the congestion, with vessels trying to make headway in every different direction. James was considered an expert driver in this respect, as he always found a path quicker than others between the coal and the hay boats, the barges and pleasure steamers, and the mass of various smaller craft filling the river.

Buoyed by a sense of increased security and an ability to work unlimited hours for fairer rewards, James and Mary had more children over the next ten years. Janie always said that she could hardly ever remember a time when her mother was not showing with child. Lucy, Florence, Alfred and Joseph all survived into childhood, however the last baby, who never had a name, was stillborn. Mary, aged 41 at the time, didn't recover from the traumatic birth and died a couple of days later in 1867.

James was left distraught with six children to support, although Edward was now 17 and halfway through his own lighterman's apprenticeship. Ten-year-old Janie and various neighbours took on the burden of looking after the brood of young children while James and Edward were at work. Nell Bradshaw never met Mary Bradshaw, her grandmother, but she felt she knew her intimately because her father and grandfather kept her alive by always speaking of her. Their love and admiration for the woman was obvious. Edward's boat, when he finally got it, was named the *Mary Bradshaw*.

Despite the hardships of raising the children, the Bradshaw family were managing well during their first year without a mother. With two wages coming into the house now, they could afford to move around in Sleaford Street, each time achieving slightly more space for the growing family. Janie, despite not having reached her 13th year, became a tenacious mother figure. She, her brother and her father battled against the odds to raise, feed and nourish their young charges; however, one fateful day, father and son quarrelled badly, and it would be many years before they were reunited. More damaging, though, was the impact the rift had on the family.

Nell's grandfather claimed that he threw his son out because he was drinking too much and coming home the worse for wear; her father said it had stemmed from the hanging of a Fenian. Nell deduced it was a combination of many factors. The two men missed Mary terribly: James had lost a wife and Edward a mother. The balance of family life had been upset radically. Edward had money in his pocket and believed he should spend it how he pleased. Down the years, the family said he resented having to spend the majority of his wages on feeding and clothing his young siblings. He was at an age when he felt he could stand up to his father. James knew that income could fluctuate, indeed disappear, and felt that his son should help support the family and conserve anything he had left over for less certain times. James, a moderate drinker, was also only too aware of the perils that could befall someone who developed a taste for the ale too soon.

The incident that sparked the final row occurred one summer evening when Edward arrived home in a drunken state. He had not taken the boat out at all that day and his father demanded to know where he had been.

'I've been to see the Fenian hang,' slurred Edward, as he clattered his coins into a bowl on the table.

The hanging was the talk of London. Michael Barrett, a young Irishman, had been tried at the Old Bailey, along with others, for an explosion at Clerkenwell Prison in which several people died and one young child lost an eye. It was alleged that Barrett and others had been attempting to free some Irish nationalists from the prison. Anti-Irish feeling was running high and the young man's public hanging outside Newgate Prison was anticipated with relish by many. As usual, when Nell asked, James would not be drawn much on the subject, although he said he felt uneasy about anyone being hanged in public, Irish or not. He told Nell he doubted if Barrett was ever guilty anyway: the frenzy surrounding the incident meant no one in authority was really focused on him receiving a fair trial.

Although public hanging had been abolished before Nell was born it was very real to her, such was its impact on previous generations. More often than not, the condemned men and women came from the community she had grown up in and in earlier days were being executed for offences she knew were easily committed during hard times: chiefly, the purloining of food. For Nell's father and his father, and everyone else's fathers and grandfathers whom they knew, hanging was a very real spectre – always there in the background. Their everyday conversation was peppered with sayings that stemmed from those very fears, things like, 'I'll swing for her, I will,' and 'You'll 'ang for this,' or 'It was like a noose round my neck,' and ''E's one for the gallows.' Nell could not have known that the hangman would figure in the life of the Bradshaws once more before her life was over.

What was said between James and Edward that night only they know. They may well have come to blows. Whatever happened, things were said and done that neither man could easily forgive. The ensuing rift was of the sort that can only afflict a father-and-son relationship. There was no woman to bang pig-heads together, although young Janie did her level best. Edward moved into a separate house along the street and did not speak to his father for nearly 20 years, even though they saw each other almost every day. All communication went through Janie and the other children. From the day of Michael Barrett's hanging, Edward publicly and privately disowned any Irish blood that may have travelled through his veins.

Edward continued to contribute to the family coffers, but Janie was struggling to keep the family together. Her father worked from dawn to dusk and sometimes at night as well. She had to prepare his food after making the children dinner, washing them and putting them to sleep. She was still a child herself. Years later, when James was telling young Nell about those difficult times, he recalled how sometimes Janie's head would drop into the broth she had prepared as exhaustion rendered her unconscious.

In the late summer of 1870, little Florence, James Bradshaw's youngest daughter at four years of age, complained to Janie of stomach cramps. Half an hour later, she collapsed into her bed following a violent attack of diarrhoea. The poor child tossed and turned and sweated and moaned. Janie panicked; she knew the symptoms. A few years earlier, there had been a cholera outbreak in Battersea and scores of youngsters in the streets around the river were lost to the disease. Families had locked their doors in case the germs were hanging in the air, waiting to strike in their house. She remembered all too well her mother supervising the constant washing of hands and her panicking at every sign of perspiration or fever, and the hushed conversations between her parents about which local children had succumbed to the disease.

Mary Bradshaw had known the likely cause of this terrible ailment was the stinking river and the general sanitary conditions. To her, it stood to reason that human waste being openly dumped and stored would be a breeding ground for germs, so Mary was quick to latch on to the use of soap.

Until the Government abolished the tax on soap, it was a luxury item that neither the Bradshaws nor any other poor Battersea family could afford. As the price fell, a bar of Pears became the most important non-food item on Mary's limited shopping list. She instilled in her sceptical husband and the children the need to wash their hands regularly and always before eating or handling food. She was fastidious about it. Janie ensured that the family's washing habits were kept up after her mother's death and that excrement was kept out of the house, but she still worried that her father brought home the gut-churning stench of the river each night. That was his smell, always had been.

The doctor came to see Florence as darkness fell, and James arrived home soon after. Her fever had not abated and she was now suffering from muscle spasms. The doctor said it looked like cholera but told her it might not be, as he had not seen many cases that year. He said the following 12 hours would be crucial. And they were. With her family around her, little Florence slipped in and out of consciousness. Her skin started to take on a blue tinge in front of them. James thought this was a good sign: he believed it meant the blood was returning to her white face. Janie knew different. Florence died three and a half hours after the doctor left, promising to return in the morning.

James was devastated; the last time he had seen his daughter – the previous day – she had been fine: full of life and playing hopscotch in the road with the other children. Now, that life had been sucked out of her without any warning at all and with grotesque speed.

When the doctor returned, he did not seem surprised to find Florence's lifeless body laid out before him and her devastated family, red-eyed and traumatised, sitting around her. He told them that she must be buried quickly to avoid the spread of disease. He then looked at Lucy, Florence's older sister by 18 months. 'I think we need to get this young lady into hospital for her own safety,' he announced. Lucy began to cry, clinging on to Janie's leg. Her big sister followed the doctor outside.

'She ain't got it too, 'as she, doctor? Please say she ain't got it.'

'We have to be careful. The cholera is in the house. We need to isolate the little girl.'

'What about the boys?'

'They're boys and they're older. They look strong to me. But, to be safe, if you have a friend or neighbour who will take them in that would be advisable.'

On the way to the London Fever Hospital in Islington, Janie took Alfred and Joseph down to Edward's house and told him he would have to look after them. There was no question of a neighbour caring for them – however neighbourly, nobody would take in children from a house where cholera had just struck. Janie comforted her young sister, assuring Lucy that the doctor wanted to isolate her from the germs and that she would be home in a couple of days. Everything would be all right.

As Lucy walked up the steps, Janie noticed the large patch of sweat on the back of her frock. She realised, with a sickly pang in her stomach, that her last remaining little sister would never be coming home again.

III

The Lightermen

Even at this desperate time in the life of the Battersea Bradshaws, father and son remained so stubborn they would not meet. Edward did not attend the funerals of his two baby sisters and James would not visit Alfie and Joseph, his youngest sons, whilst they were living under Edward's roof. Janie despaired. Her family had been devastated in a matter of days and the two men she looked up to were behaving like a couple of truculent children. Instead of comforting her, they added to her grief.

When Edward delivered his eleven- and nine-year-old brothers to the Industrial Home for Outcast Boys in Lambeth after only having them with him for a month or two, Janie decided she too could not speak to him again. He had not even consulted her or her father. By this time, James was so battered and damaged by the events of the last couple of years that he believed they were maybe better off in the home – at least until all traces of cholera had been wiped out in the area.

Janie was even more heartbroken when young Joseph returned home a few months later without his brother. Alfie liked the home and they had fixed him up with work at a factory up at Nine Elms making belt buckles. In less than a year, he had grown into a little man. By the time he was 14 years old, Alfie had become self-sufficient: he was versed in the ways of the world and had stopped visiting his family in Sleaford Street. Cholera hadn't killed him, but he too was lost to the family. The last anyone heard of him was years later when there were reports that he had married and had children and lived somewhere in north London. Maybe. Neither Janie nor indeed anyone else in the family ever saw Alfie again after he was 16. There hadn't been a row, nor were there any hard feelings – the wind of necessity had merely blown him off onto a different course. In later life, Nell often bemoaned the fact that the family had made no real effort to find Alfie, or he them, but she too did nothing to remedy the situation. Maybe she could not. In an age before telephones and directory enquiries, home ownership and accessible electoral registers, estranged family members could often go missing for years. If one wanted to disappear altogether, it was less of a challenge to do so.

As soon as young Joseph could fend for himself, Janie decided to leave home. She had been like a wife to her father and a mother to her siblings; now, she wanted a life of her own. She was bitter about the estrangement of her brother and father, and she was still shell shocked at the collapse of the family unit. She also was conscious that she was reaching a point where her limited window of opportunity to marry would begin to close. Joseph was there to keep their father company and to look out for him. And Edward was living along the road – he could do his bit, although she knew he would not. For her, the house now held only painful memories. She applied for some posts in domestic service and was finally offered a job in the country home of the Nettlefold family, near Hastings on the south coast of England.

Therefore, in 1875, at 18 years of age – but feeling she had already lived a lifetime – Janie kissed her father and brother goodbye (separately) and went to live in the country seat of a northern industrialist who had made his money manufacturing nails and screws. She returned to Battersea rarely, to attend the very occasional funeral or wedding. Hastings was not even 100 miles away, but it could have been 500: because of the expense, visits up and down the railway line were not undertaken lightly. In time, Janie met a Romford man by the name of Staines, also a servant, and they married and raised a large family. She bore no real affection or attachment for the place of her birth and childhood, and spent her remaining 70 years counting her lucky stars that she lived in such a happy, gentle and healthy part of the country.

Meanwhile, the soldiers of the British Empire were continually fighting small wars in colonial outposts in the far corners of the world. The Empire's appetite for young, fit recruits was forever growing. Young Joseph signed up as an infantryman just as soon as he could and by the year 1881 was seeing action in South Africa in what became known as the First Boer War.

Joseph was the first Battersea Bradshaw to travel abroad (other than from Ireland) and the first to fight for his Queen and country. He was also the first to die in conflict: the injuries he sustained in the notorious Battle of Majuba Hill killing him a few days later. Majuba was a terrible defeat for the army. The Boers had routed the British soldiers as they came up Majuba Hill and many had died falling over each other as they tumbled down the mountain in sheer panic.

It became an even lonelier and sadder life for James Bradshaw, who had always done his best for his family. In the space of fifteen years, he had lost his wife in childbirth, two of his children to cholera and another to a crude Boer bullet in a far-off land. He had been so proud when Joseph had stood there in the room, resplendent in his uniform. He was proud for his son and he was proud for himself. He felt that by producing a son who was about to serve a Queen and country that had taken him and Mary in, he had repaid the debt and that his adopted home had now fully embraced him. He had not really considered that his son would need to lay down his life and he was sure Joseph had not either. It was this naivety that hurt more than anything. His beloved and loyal daughter had moved to the countryside, a son had disappeared almost off the face of the earth and his eldest son, although he still saw him most days on the river, looked through him as if he did not exist. All he had worked and struggled for seemed lost. He sometimes wondered if he and Mary would have been better off staying in Ireland and perishing.

But he took solace in his work and was out on the river in his barge more than ever before. By now, he was one of the oldest men under oars and everyone knew him. They said he could drive his barge better than any man on the river. He was earning reasonable money and, with nobody to spend it on, started to put some by for the first time in his life. That was another first in all of his tough years – having slightly more money than he needed to survive.

* * *

Annie Morgan lived in Savona Street, a road that ran parallel to Sleaford Street. Such was the proximity of their two homes, Edward could have thrown a lump of coal from his house and it would have landed in Annie's yard. Maybe he did. Her father, too, had arrived in Battersea from Ireland at about the same time as

James and Mary Bradshaw and had found work as a coachman. Annie was one of eleven children and Edward knew them all – as a child, he had played with the older Morgans in the streets and the railway yards. Together, the children from all the streets would climb up the steps to the main road, cross over by the Dogs Home and walk down into Battersea Park – their slice of the country and the exotic in their midst.

When she was 16 years old, Annie went into service with a family in one of the big houses on Cheyne Walk, just over Battersea Bridge. As she returned home from work, Edward would spy her through the window of the Duke of York pub, where he was having his first pint of mild in the evening. As she hurried past, Edward would stare at her, pointedly daring Annie to return his gaze such was the immediate attraction he felt. But she never let her line of vision veer, having been taught by her mother to ignore public houses and more so the people who frequented them. Edward resolved further to attract her attention. He started by rapping on the window one day as she passed and was encouraged when she returned his wave. He then began taking his drink outside, so he could waylay her and make conversation, even when it was winter and was cold. And finally he asked her to walk out with him.

Annie was small but big-boned, like all the Morgans, but it was her high cheekbones and sultry eyes that particularly attracted Edward. He could see, too, that she was a buxom girl, despite the layers of clothing and shawls she wore that did their best to hide such alluring features. In later years, the high cheekbones would accentuate her sinking eyes and give her hookish nose extra prominence – her habit of sitting in her chair and moving her head to the side so she could hear conversation with her good ear gave her the air of a mildly alarmed woodpecker. But in her youth and prime, as far as Edward was concerned, she was a beautiful peahen. For her part, she knew that her admirer had steady work as a river man and she thought of him as a good-looking fellow. When he suggested marriage in the summer of 1876, she accepted. She was only 17 and he was 26.

Together they set up home in Edward's rooms in Sleaford Street. Children came along at regular intervals soon after and in short order: Bill in 1878, Annie in 1883, Tom in 1885, Ellen (Nell) in 1888, Margaret (Maggs) in 1891, Sam in 1893, Edward (Teddy) in 1896 and finally Henry in 1897. Annie died in infancy and two others were stillborn, therefore Bill, Tom, Nell, Margaret, Sam, Teddy and Henry formed the core of the next generation of Battersea Bradshaws.

Nell remembered her early childhood as the happiest of times. Her father worked hard and drank hard, but there was always food on the table and a farthing here or a halfpenny there for sweets. Life was good. Her grandfather's early troubled life of starvation and strife seemed as far away as the old Kings and Queens of England about whom she was taught in the little school in Sleaford Street that her father was paying the few pennies for her to attend.

All the children were left pretty much to their own devices. They banded together in the streets, wandering in and out of each other's houses as if the road was one long dormitory and everything belonged to everyone. They played street games, such as hopscotch, skipping, marbles, spinning the hoop, Jimmy Jimmy Knacker, football, cricket and, when feeling particularly mischievous, Knock Down Ginger, and the time flew by. At weekends, they'd wander into Battersea Park and watch the aristocrats in their posh clothes trotting their sleek horses around the tracks and generally showing off. Up at the bandstand, they'd run around between the seats, generally making a nuisance of themselves as the well-dressed grown-ups out for their Sunday constitutional tried to shoo them away so they could enjoy the brass band. Best of all was hiding among the bushes around the boating lake and spying on the courting couples on their skiffs as they snatched kisses, sometimes more. Battersea Park was a godsend to the kids. Few other poor communities in London had such a rich and varied environment in which to play so close to home, although the attitudes of the keepers and their constant brinkmanship suggested that the park might not really have been intended for the children.

Nell did not know until much later that her father and grandfather had not spoken for so many years because old James Bradshaw had lived with her from as early as she could remember. In 1888, the year of Nell's birth, he had, in fact, only just moved in. The previous year, he had had to accept that, at 73 years old, with his old muscles weakening and his back creaking, he could no longer row the *Galway Bay* up and down the Thames and load and unload cargoes. With great regret and sadness, he gave the boat to a young friend and was forced to become a boarder in a single room above an ironmonger's shop on Battersea Park Road. He had conserved a small amount of money from which he had calculated he could eke out this smaller rent for two to three years hence. He hoped he would die before his savings ran out, otherwise it was the workhouse for him and the thought of that filled him with dread. It was here you were sent when you had no means of support and could not earn a living either through unemployment, ill health or old age. It was a miserable existence made worse by the knowledge that when you went in, you were very, very unlikely to ever come out.

It was Annie who brought the two men back together, and it was a story she often told. She had seen James in the street and had stopped to talk with him, as she always did, dismissing her husband's objections to their contact as childish and churlish. The old man told her that he was despairing, that the money he had saved was close to running dry, and he would then be faced with the real prospect of the workhouse. Like hanging before it, the workhouse held the greatest fear for the poor people of London and beyond.

'We shall 'ave to take 'im in,' Annie announced to her husband when recounting to him the meeting in the street.

'We shall not. I ain't spoken to the man for 20 years. I'll not 'ave 'im under any roof of mine.'

'The old fella is past 70 years of age. It won't be for long. Blow me if 'e lasts more than a month or two. 'Ave some mercy in yer soul for yer own bloody farver.'

Remarkably, an accommodation was reached and somehow father and son patched up their differences. The reconciliation when it happened was so quick and painless it made the previous 20 years appear even more pathetic than they were. James was far from infirm and for the next 13 years he looked after the children whilst Edward worked the river and his wife went cleaning. The old man may not have been able to row a heavy barge up and down the Thames, but he retained his energy and zest for life and remained active until his dying day. When Nell came in from school, he would sit her down and ask her exactly what she had learnt that day, not because he was checking up on her but because he was hungry to learn himself. Over the years on the river, he had picked up some basic reading skills and had learnt to recognise the names of the many countries and ports that sent goods into the London docks. He taught himself to read and write in earnest, starting with his Bible, in his 70s. It was a long struggle, with no formal tuition, but he finally got there. When the public library on Lavender Hill opened up, James was in his element, walking over there each afternoon to sit and read to his heart's content. He said it was the greatest gift 'they' had ever given to the working man. He was full of wonder for the very concept of a library. 'You should see all the books, Nellie girl, and the chairs. Chairs everywhere. They let you sit down and read. Read as much as you like. For as long as you like.'

James would devour the newspaper in the library and then come home and relay the day's news to anyone who would listen. The Bradshaws were extraordinarily well informed for a poor, ill-educated Battersea family. Nell can remember her grandfather giving daily bulletins on the progress of the Second Boer War, which culminated in the famous Relief of Mafeking, an event that prompted much celebrating on the streets of London (forever after, Nell would describe any hint of a crowd or disorder with a dramatic 'It's like the bleedin' Relief of Mafeking out there'). Old James had become a curiosity in the area, as here was a man who was born before the Duke of Wellington defeated Napoleon at Waterloo keeping everyone in touch with world events. Neighbours and friends would come to the house to listen to James and his news, and he found himself in demand for advice on anything from medical ailments to deciphering official letters. The community assumed that age equalled wisdom and in James Bradshaw's case it probably did.

Father and son became close again in these years and it was as if their period of estrangement had never happened. Nell believed that the row saddened and embarrassed them both and that is why it was never mentioned, not because of any fears of reigniting the quarrel.

Soon after Grandpa James had moved in and while Nell was still a babe in arms, events on the river united father and son in a common purpose. Despite the huge growth in the docks up and down the river and evidence of the country's growing consumption of imported goods, from exotic fruit to herbs and spices, those working on the river remained a largely poorly paid, poorly treated and undernourished community. James and Edward were better off than many as lightermen, but they, especially James, were sensitive to the injustice of the working practices on the river. The dockers got the worst deal by far. This huge army of men living or gathered by the river were forced to wait for the 'call-on' each day to see who, if any, would be working and bringing home food that evening. It was a humiliating and soul-destroying ritual for the dockers. The suited, well-groomed plumper men from the harbour and shipping companies strolled around among them selecting workers from the hopeful as if they were cattle in a market.

The call-on sometimes descended into a mass brawl as desperate people fought one another to get picked: it was not unheard of for men to be seriously injured, and once or twice dockers were killed at call-on time – 'Treat a man as a beast and he will become a beast,' James often said. If you were 'lucky' enough to be selected, the company could then hire you for an hour or two only, if they so wished, pay you a few shillings and send you on your way. It was a sorry situation of exploitation and greed on the part of the companies, and it was not until some well-educated activists came among the dockers and told them that they had rights and that they did not need to be abused in this way that an air of discontent and rebellion spread up and down the river.

Such was the gulf between rich and poor that neither side really believed the situation could be any different. When they were told by these outsiders that they were being treated unjustly and that they possessed the power to change things by bartering with the only thing they had – their labour – it was a radical notion. If you knew no different and remembered even harder times, it was foreign to think of yourself as deprived. The idea that together the workers possessed this power was exhilarating and novel.

There had been a huge fuss when the 'match girls' at the Bryant & May factory went out on strike further up the river in Bow. The stories coming out of there were appalling: girls turning into haggard old women before their time due to the arduous work and the chemicals that the matches were being dipped in rotting their jawbones. As Nell grew up, her mother, Annie, would say of any elderly lady whose mouth hung open a little that she must have worked at the match factory at some time. The match girls had huge support and the factory owners met most of their demands for more humane conditions. Shortly after, the stokers and other workers at the Beckton Gas Works went out on strike to achieve an eight-hour day, and they got it too.

Edward and James had no idea exactly who organised the Dock Strike in the summer of 1889. It was a perfect example of word and bond by mouth. But Edward went to see a number of people speak, including Ben Tillett and John Burns. Tillett impressed him no end. Edward had heard Tillett suffered from a speech impediment, but on the stage he spoke with a passion and clarity that left Edward burning with the injustice of it all. Tillett made the men feel strong as they left the meetings, steeling themselves for even harder times ahead. He was born in Bristol and had worked as a shoemaker and acrobat, among other things, before coming to London and becoming a tea-cooper at the London docks. He was a working-class lad, for sure. John Burns, James guessed, had benefited from a good education, but he did not hold this against him since Burns was born in Lambeth, and Battersea was his home. James was in awe of him, as he had seen him climb onto a platform in Hyde Park and address a crowd of thousands with a voice as loud and as authoritative as any he had ever heard. Standing there in his bowler hat, and shirt and tie, James could see that the working man, for the first time, had a formidable leader who had the force of personality and charismatic presence and influence to change the status quo.

In her old age, Nell had amplified in her mind the relationship between these two men and her father. No longer were they orator and spectator, or leader and follower – they were nigh on family friends. Even years before, when John Burns became MP for Battersea and later a minister in the Liberal Government, she had often mused, 'If the worst comes to the worst, I'll pop up the road and 'ave a word with Mr Burns.' She seemed to draw some comfort from his close proximity.

The workers were demanding 'the docker's tanner': the minimum wage of 6d an hour and also a minimum of a half-day's work when hired. They were fair demands and everybody except the dock companies could see it. At call-on one morning, everybody simply refused to be called on. It had started. The stevedores and the lightermen joined the dockers without hesitation and before long groups of workers from beyond the river were downing tools and joining the protest in sympathy. As the dockers were the only men directly affected, it was a remarkable demonstration of solidarity among the poorer people of London. The competition that often soured relations between the dry dockers and the lightermen was put to one side in an effort to make the companies pay. It was a general strike in all but name.

'I don't see why you can't go to work. It's not our fight,' pleaded Annie, as Edward put on his Sunday suit in preparation for the big march in support of the strike that would parade through London that day.

'It's our fight, woman. Look at baby Nell 'ere. We 'ave to fight to feed 'er and the others. Do you think the toffs 'ave to worry about where the next meal comes from?'

'But you *were* earning. We always 'ad a meal. Now we 'ave to take charity.'

'Not for long, Annie, not for long. They will give in. Look out on the river. The goods are piling up. The fruits are going rotten. The sugar is bad. Soon, as they start going short and there is no port in their bleedin' cellars or fine cheese in their larders, you'll see, they'll pay.'

Annie did not understand or agree with it. If they 'paid', as Edward said, how did it affect them, except to put them back where they were? Her patience with the whole thing became more and more strained as the weeks went by and the strike dragged on into September. When it was finally settled and the dockers got their fairer deal, she heaved a huge sigh of relief.

The Battersea men savoured the victory and the night the strike ended was marked by late-night celebrations in the pubs and inns where the landlords were happy to grant credit, knowing they could now be sure that their customers would be able to repay. The river men had a confidence and a swagger about them after that, basking in the knowledge that they had righted a wrong. They would no longer be downtrodden. The womenfolk were not so sure.

In 1901, Grandpa Bradshaw died. He was old. Very old. Some said he was the oldest man in Battersea. Few people at the turn of the nineteenth century surpassed the three score years and ten, as James had easily. He was, in fact, 87 years of age and he was active until the morning of his death when he took to his bed feeling poorly. He had eaten a breakfast of bread, milk and cheese.

'D'you want me to stay 'ere with you, Father?' Annie asked, worried by her father-in-law's sweating brow and his greying complexion, as she laced her boots for work. Edward was already out on the barge.

'Be off with you, Annie. Nell and Tom are here; they can look after the young uns. I'm going to my bed and I'll be as right as ninepence in an hour or two.'

Annie found him dead in the afternoon when she came home from work. The children had gone to the park so the old man could sleep. Annie left him lying there until Edward arrived back from the river – the children all thought it strange that they were to carry on their business whilst their grandpa lay there dead in the corner of the room.

Nell was closer to her grandpa than any of her siblings. They spent a lot of time together and shared a thirst for knowledge. She was the only one of the grandchildren who really wanted to know and understand about his past and where he had come from. She loved listening to his stories and he loved telling her them. They had a very special bond. She was proud of his life and what he had achieved. She could see that his time and his environment had held him back, and that he was a very unusual man. He was passionate about education and believed that schooling was the only way to break free from the cycle of poverty. For him and his children those first opportunities came too late. His greatest wish was that things would be different for his grandchildren.

The family went into black when James died and were joined only days later by most of the country when Queen Victoria died too and Britain entered a long period of mourning. Nell had forever linked the passing of Queen Victoria and the death of her grandfather. As the years went by, she merged the two funerals in her mind and the period when people wore black for weeks on end. In the last decades of her life, she came to believe that the population was as upset at James's death as it was at its sovereign's. The streets of Battersea were lined six deep for his funeral, she told people in her hazy final years.

What remained crystal clear in Nell's mind was that James's body was kept in a coffin in the house for a few days, and that friends from the neighbourhood and the river came in a steady stream to pay their respects, and the misery and pain she felt when she kissed his cold forehead before the undertakers slid the lid on the coffin and took her grandfather out of the house for the last time. The family followed the horse-drawn cart that carried his body to the cemetery in two broughams pulled by horses with black plumes strapped to their manes. This is where Nell's memory becomes confused because here she remembers locals lining Battersea Park Road, heads bowed, hats pressed to chests, with police forming a human cordon to keep them on the pavements as the cortège rode past.

IV

Boy Overboard

For Edward Bradshaw, 1901 was a tumultuous year. His father died, his Queen died and a singular piece of luck would change his life for ever.

Early one crisp morning, a worker down on the moorings addressed him as he untied the *Mary Bradshaw*. 'You 'eard about the goings on last night, I expects?'

'No, my friend, and what was that?'

'Man overboard. Real toff. Son of a lord, they say. Drunk as lords, I say. Skylarking on one of the old steamers. 'E went over just around 'ere. 'E's not been washed up anywhere round these parts yet. But I'm keeping me eyes peeled. The family are up in arms and are off'rin' a big reward.'

''Ow much?'

'Dunno. Ask up at the wharf. The lord and his wife 'ave got 'alf of London looking out for the poor wretch.'

Battersea people were familiar with the pleasure boats that

ploughed up and down the Thames carrying the young and wealthy as they drank and danced the night away. It was not unusual that high spirits got the better of them and they occasionally splashed into the river – sometimes intentionally, sometimes not. They would normally be hauled back on board, or get fished out of the water by a passing waterman, or were even able to swim to the shore suddenly sober.

The following evening, Edward picked up an evening newspaper from the boy outside the pub and took it home for Nell to read to him. 'Is there anything there about the young lord who fell drunk into the river?' he asked.

Nell found the story and read aloud to her father. There was no mention of a reward. Edward had smelled money. He remembered the tragedy two decades earlier of the *Princess Alice*, the steamboat that collided with another large vessel up the river at Woolwich. He had only been under oars a couple of years when it happened. The *Princess Alice* had been packed with day-trippers coming back from Sheerness and they were almost home when the steamer ploughed into a coal ship named the *Bywell Castle*. The *Alice* was soon underwater and the 700-odd passengers found themselves fighting for their lives as the sun went down. Few were saved, the greedy Thames claiming at least 600 of their number – a domestic disaster of massive proportions. But it wasn't the terrible loss of life that Edward thought about that evening, it was that the Thames barge drivers were paid five shillings a man for every body they pulled out of the river. He can remember reproaching himself for wishing the disaster had happened when he was out on the river and nearer to his home.

Edward knew the sets of the tides and currents of the Thames on his stretch of the river better than most and when he heard that the water had still not surrendered the body the following day, he set out to look in a few places he felt the unfortunate young man could have ended up. There was an inlet across the river, over by the Embankment, where the currents carried wood, silt, excrement and the flotsam and jetsam of the Thames. Like a floating dump, the debris accumulated there and it was rarely, if ever, cleared. You could smell this cesspool long before you could see it and large black rats managed to forage and scuttle across the surface without sinking into the water. He steered his barge into the bay and had poked around with his sweep for only seconds when he saw the young man's body floating face down, with his legs caught between two pegs that had once supported a small pier. He was amazed that nobody had observed the corpse in two days. Looking around to see if anyone from the street was watching, he took some sacking from his barge and covered the body from view before pushing the boat out river and away with his oar. He had not planned to do this. He simply did it.

'Nell, anything in this paper about that toff?' he asked, slapping a rolled-up newspaper onto the table when he arrived in from work. Nell could find no mention and her father grunted.

This ritual continued for two or three more days until one evening Nell read a small piece ending with: 'The Earl and his wife are offering a reward of 200 guineas to anyone who can discover the body of their lost son.' That night, Edward confided in his wife about his gruesome discovery and his subsequent actions. She received the news with a horror that took him by surprise.

'You've found the poor boy? Why 'aven't you 'anded 'im over to 'is poor parents?'

'I was waiting to see if they put up a reward.'

Annie looked at her husband in a new light and did not like what she saw. 'And you've left the poor boy – somebody's son – floating there in the muck? 'Ow could you? That could 'ave bin our Bill. It's wicked. That's what it is. Wicked.'

'Well, it's not our Bill. It's a toff. And 'e's dead. Long dead before I finds him. And you won't be complaining, Annie, when I empties 200 guineas out on this table.'

'That'll be the devil's shilling and I'll not be taking it. Mark my words.'

Women can be funny, Edward thought, not seeing any harm in what he was doing. He had found the body and was just a little late in telling anyone. What was the problem? He hadn't killed anybody.

That evening, as the orange sun slotted into the river on the horizon, he drove the barge across the water and removed the sacking from the body with his sweep before hauling the drowned boy onto his barge by hooking his arms under the corpse's shoulders and heaving him on board. He'd seen dead bodies before, and drowned ones at that, but this young man was already in a sorry state. The skin had rotted, or had perhaps been chewed at by rats, because parts of the cheekbone and jaw were exposed. Edward could not look for too long once he'd noticed the empty socket where an eyeball had been. He quickly covered the dead boy's face with his cap, bracing himself against the urge to vomit, and steered into a current to take his find to the police. A day later, when his name was listed in the newspaper as 'the eagle-eyed waterman who discovered the young man's body' and Nell read this aloud, he wore a smile of satisfaction – but not as big as the one he wore a few days later when a postal order for 200 guineas was delivered to his door.

The reward was an enormous amount of money. Edward would be fortunate to earn £50 in an entire year. It was certainly a bigger sum than had ever been possessed by a Bradshaw, but Annie was not sharing in her husband and children's celebratory mood. Her sense of shame, alarm and deep foreboding intensified when Edward announced, 'Well, I can give up work now, for sure.'

'You could give up work for four or five years maybe,' said Annie, 'but what after that?'

'I won't need to work so hard then. The children will be grown up,' protested Edward. Annie pointed out that young Henry was four years old – in five years' time, he would be nine, and that could hardly be counted as 'grown up'. But her husband was not listening. He could have used the money to change the family's life – that was what upset Annie more than anything. They could have moved out of London and bought a smallholding in Kent, or even a public house down in the countryside near his sister, Janie, but he was not interested. He was nearly an old man, he reasoned; too old to be going off buying pubs or farms. The money would be used to ease his retirement and make their lives more comfortable. No workhouse for any of them, he declared.

Sadly, Annie's worst fears were soon realised. Her husband merely did less work and spent more time in the pubs, gin palaces and inns.

Bill, their eldest son, had already passed out as a lighterman. He was assigned to a master lighterman and he took over much of his father's regular work and river relationships, and became the first of the children to leave home. Bolstered by his own growing income, he married Dolly, his childhood sweetheart, who was earning a living herself at the Peak Frean biscuit factory at Bermondsey. They moved to the ground floor of some smarter newly built three-storey houses off the Battersea Park Road, close to Battersea Park, and although they remained in close proximity to Sleaford Street they were never really at the centre of the family again. Nell found this sad, as she looked up to both her older brothers, Tom and Bill, and did not like to see the family dissipating in any way. Little did she appreciate that this was only the beginning.

Bill may have seen it coming and got out in the nick of time, but the rest of the family had to sit and watch as their father's personality changed before their eyes. He had always liked a drink, but he was no different to the other working fathers in Battersea, who drank regularly after work a couple of days a week and to excess on a Friday and Saturday night. They'd seen him drunk, but he had never been belligerent or violent in front of them. Indeed, the drink agreed with him, they thought. Sometimes, he'd come in from the Duchess of York and throw his coins in the air, sending the kids scurrying across the floor for a tanner or threepenny bit. Other times, he'd regale them with stories about the night's events and the torrid marital problems of old Bert and Gertie Leverett. Annie would chide him for discussing the private business of his neighbours, but the children loved it.

However, once he had the 'reward money', as Annie began to scornfully refer to the windfall, he started to visit the pubs in the daytime and then again in the evening. The marriage became strained. Edward did not share his fortune with the family in any significant way. Annie thought they'd at least be able to go off on a holiday at the seaside or see her relations in Nottingham and Scotland, but Edward was not interested.

There was never any shortage of 'pals' to drink with but, as Annie often noted, 'Let's see if they're still so fond of you when the reward money's gone.' She feared that by coming off the river he would lose his ability to make a living when he needed to again, as he surely would. And she would tell him this frequently.

'You're driving me to drink, woman,' was his closing refrain as he smacked his cap down on his head and threw his jacket on before slamming the door and heading off to the pub. When he came home, he was more than ready to resume the argument. Annie knew then was not the time to engage with him.

Nell can remember only too vividly the first and only time she saw her father hit her mother. It was early in 1903 and she was kneeling on the cold floor as she bathed young Henry in the tub whilst her

mother walked around them, putting soup on the table for the rest
of the children who were filing in for tea after playing outside in the
street. Edward came in from the sailor's club, where he could get a
drink in the afternoons, and immediately started a row.

'Why do you look at me like that?' he challenged.

'Like what?'

'Like this!' He pulled a long, disapproving face, seemingly
imitating his wife's expression.

'You've been drinkin'.'

'Yes, I 'ave. Is that an 'anging offence now?'

'No, but don't you think it would be a good idea to go to work?
When was the last time you took yer boat out?'

'Don't you think I've worked 'ard all me life? Worked like a nigger,
me, since I was a boy. Why is it such a crime for me to sit back awhile
and spend some of the money that I've toiled for so 'ard?'

'Toiled for so 'ard? You call what you did to get the reward
money toiling 'ard? I don't.'

Nell heard the crack of flesh on bone first and then from her
position at floor level saw her mother's heels rock back as if in slow
motion and then the rest of her body topple over backwards.
Before she was able to jump up and run to her mother and cradle
her unconscious head in her arms, she heard the sound of the door
slamming.

'It's the Irish in 'im. 'E can't 'elp it,' Annie explained to Nell
later, as she sat in her chair recovering from Edward's left hook to
her jaw. Although she was trying to protect her children from
thinking the worst of their father, she really did believe what she
had told them. There was a school of thought, bizarrely often
upheld by Irish men and women themselves, that the Irish race
were either alcoholics or alcoholics-in-waiting; that, should the
means present themselves, they would drink themselves into
oblivion and death at the earliest opportunity. Edward himself

would have subscribed to this theory, though he never considered himself to have Irish blood in him.

Edward never mentioned the incident and neither did Annie or Nell. Henry was the only other witness, but he was oblivious, being just a baby. Mother and daughter discussed it with each other, though, but Annie wanted to play it down and insisted that Bill and Tom were not told. 'I don't want *them* not talking to their father for 20 years, do I?'

Annie never told Nell the full story behind the drowned body and how her husband had hidden it to maximise the possibility of a reward. She did not want her daughter to think any less of her father than perhaps she now already did.

Tom was still at home and had found work as a riveter in the railway yards, but he yearned to leave Battersea and travel the world. Like Nell, he had been a keen scholar and enjoyed reading, either devouring boys' comics about the great explorers and travellers or poring over maps and atlases at great length. He was disappointed at being too young for the Boer War, seeing this as a travel opportunity missed rather than a potential threat to his life. He courted excitement. He augmented his income by becoming a runner for one of the many street bookies that operated in the area. With his pals, he often took the tram or train into London and came home to tell Nell about their tricks and japes in the West End. By the age of 18, Tom had outgrown Battersea and had rejected all suggestions by his father and older brother, Bill, that it was high time he 'got under oars' on the river.

Nell loved Tom in a way she didn't any of her other siblings. Bill was that much older and had therefore always been more of a father figure. The others were all younger and, increasingly, Nell became a mother to them all. So Tom was the only one who shared a childhood on equal terms with her. They were as close as a brother and sister could be. She loved Tom's sense of fun, his wit, his refusal to fall out with anyone. She adored the way he looked, and she knew that he would be one of those boys that would be able to have his pick of the girls. He didn't need to work at it; his cheeky smile and deep-blue eyes saw to that. He had a head of tousled brown hair that possessed its own mind – the more his mother combed and brushed it, the more it stuck up. And soap didn't seem to work on Tom – again, the more she scrubbed at his collar, the more dirt he would accumulate next time. But he still looked great to Nell and she treasured him. In turn, he loved her loyalty to the family and her strength. He saw how, as his father faltered and his mother took on more and more, Nell held the family together at the expense of her own life. He knew he could not ever do the same. But he feared for his sister, worrying that history might repeat itself and she could end up having the burden of raising a young family whilst still a young girl, like his aunt Janie had.

Nell remembers one particular day when she went to more places with Tom than she had been in the rest of her life. They were both teenagers and Tom suggested they go train hopping. 'Come on, gal. Let's see the world. England at least!' He bought two tickets for them at Clapham Junction and from there they travelled down to Brighton. A few gulps of sea air later and they were back inland at Lewes, and then over to Haywards Heath, and then back up to Victoria Station, and then a walk down the Embankment and home. At each railway station en route, Tom would jump out of the carriage and then jump back in again just as the guard would wave his green flag.

'What you playing at, Tom?' Nell asked.

'I've got to say I've been to a place, Nell. Not just passed through.'

It was only when they were back at home, telling Annie and the little ones of their eventful day, that Tom revealed they had just travelled the length and breadth of the south of England on two halfpenny platform tickets.

Then there was the time that the policeman brought Tom back to the house, clasping him by the ear. 'I caught him and his chum in the park. He'd swum across to the island on the lake and was trying to steal the heron's eggs.'

'No, I never, Mum. I was trying to get a better look at the bird. That's all.'

Luckily for Tom his father was out.

'Thank you, sir,' said Annie. 'You can be sure I'll be giving him an 'iding now and 'e'll be 'avin anover when his old man gets 'ome, for sure.'

The policeman let go of Tom's ear and shoved him through the door. Annie thanked the officer once more and assured him that Tom would not be allowed into Battersea Park again to bother the poor old herons. When she walked back into the room, she put her hands on her hips and fixed her glare on Tom, as a puddle of water from his clothes formed around him. Tom figured that if she was going to belt him, she would have done so by now.

'Don't tell Dad,' he implored.

'Oo were you with, boy?'

'Jimmy Lock – he swam one way, I swam the other. The copper could only catch one of us.'

The thought of Tom and Jimmy getting caught on the island, with the policeman on the shore, demanding they swim back to him, flashed through Annie's mind and she could not stop herself laughing. Nell joined in, and then young Maggs, before Tom allowed himself to do so as well.

'Go on, get out of those togs before your farver comes 'ome. And stop knocking around with that Jimmy Lock – 'e leads you into bad ways.' In Battersea, it was always someone else's child that led yours astray; that was a given.

When Tom told his mother and Nell one night that he was leaving home the following morning to seek his fortune in Wales of all places, they laughed at first – until they realised he was serious.

'There's plenty of work in them coal mines, Mum.'

'But you've got a job 'ere up the bloody road!'

'The money's better. I'll be able to save my fare for Australia or America.'

'It's coal they're digging up, Tom, not gold,' interjected Nell.

Tom smiled at his sister's ability to inject a bit of cold reality into any situation, but she was missing the point. Tom wanted to go. Foreign lands beckoned and Wales was a start. There was no ocean between them and England, but they talked funny. He was past reading about travel and adventure in the *Boy's Own Paper*; he needed to live it.

The following morning, Annie packed up some clothes for Tom, and Nell handed him some sandwiches wrapped in her handkerchief.

'A proper little Dick Whittington you are,' Nell said, trying to hold back the tears.

Edward stood by awkwardly, saying very little, conscious that his wife and eldest daughter may have felt that Tom's departure could have had something to do with him.

''Ow long will it take you on the train?' asked Annie.

'I'm walking, Mum.'

Edward shook his head, as his son stood there laughing and brimming with hope and adventure. 'And how long do you think that's going to take you, son?'

'Two weeks,' returned Tom, who had it all worked out.

'Well, you be careful, son,' Edward pulled the teenager towards him with a handshake and almost embraced him.

Nell hugged her brother, knowing she would see him in the future but never again would they live together as brother and sister under the same roof. No more pulling faces at each other behind their parents' backs. No more sharing books and magazines. They all followed him out into the street and then out onto the main road, where he walked up towards Battersea Bridge, turning around every few seconds to wave goodbye to his family. Just before he disappeared from sight, Nell noticed him take her handkerchief from his pocket, untie the knot and bite into one of the sandwiches. There were only 200 miles to go.

V

The Greedy River

With Bill and Tom having left home and with her husband's reward money dwindling, Annie was forced to take on more cleaning jobs, as well as taking in ironing to supplement the increasingly erratic household purse. She crossed the river early each morning to clean in the big houses in Chelsea and then collected washing from other houses to iron and deliver the following day. Annie had not expected to have to throw herself into such arduous work as she approached her sixth decade, at a time when many of her peers were succumbing to disease and wear and tear. She began to resent her husband with more intensity each day. He had been forced to work the river again, but, as she had predicted, he had lost his edge and was certainly not prepared to put in the long hours – the call of the pub controlled him now. She could not help but envy the families she charred for on Cheyne Walk and down the King's Road: servants and maids at their beck and call, sweeping staircases, the sheer amount of space in their towering houses, and most of all the life of leisure the ladies of the houses seemed to lead. They had gentlemen callers, took strolls in parks and tea and coffee, and enjoyed 'glorious' nights out at the theatre. She did not resent the ladies – they were born into what they were born into and she was born into what she was. It was nobody's fault, but it didn't stop her envying them. The breadth of the River Thames was all that separated them geographically, but socially and economically they were continents apart.

The change in circumstances meant Nell had to take on the role of mother to Margaret, Sam, Teddy and young Henry even more. She left school earlier than she should have and instead had the task of raising and dressing the children each morning so *they* could attend school. Then she'd do the washing and ironing that her mother had been unable to finish and deliver it to the customers on foot. She'd then hurry back over Battersea Bridge to make tea for the children and again for her mother and father in the evening. When her father went out to the pub again, his appetite sated, the family would sit and talk, and most nights Nell would read to them all before they went to bed. Like her grandfather before her, if there were no books to hand she'd read from the newspaper, trying to find the stories that might hold some interest for her brothers and sister.

Although she always ensured she was in bed, either asleep or pretending to be asleep, when Edward came stumbling in after the pubs had chucked out, Nell could not help but hear the ritual that was played out most nights. In two rooms in Sleaford Street, privacy was not an option. Edward would fall into bed with Annie and he would make it clear what he wanted, ignoring her heavy breathing, which she hoped would signify she was in a deep slumber. It made Nell wince to hear her mother gently coaxing him and doing whatever it was she did under the rustling blanket to quieten him down and send him off to sleep so soundly. Nell resolved she would never allow a man to treat her in such a way, and she never did.

Nell's life was hard and busy, but she delighted in her younger brothers and sister and watched fascinated as their individual characters developed. Margaret was three years Nell's junior, which is a big gap when you're 15 going on 30 and your sister is 12. She was like Tom in some ways, inasmuch as she was cheeky and loved her fun, but she had her father in her too and could display a temper and awkwardness.

Maggs, as she became known as she moved into her teens, grew into a very pretty girl, with her high cheekbones and blonde bouncing curls. The local boys were beating a path to her door from a very early age. Nell did what she could to keep them at bay because she knew what could happen to young girls who were not wise to boys and their ways, but Maggs would have none of it, being cocksure about herself and sometimes dismissive of her older sister and her matronly ways. Soon, it was not just boys who were presenting a threat. Nell recalls the day well when she and her mother marched down to a photographic studio on Battersea Rise and gave the man 'what for' because he had invited young Maggs to his studio alone for some 'portrait work'.

Brother Sam was altogether quieter and more timid. The gamut of childhood illnesses – measles, mumps, influenza and rickets, to name but a few – had left him alive (unlike many of his peers) but had rendered him weak and less adventurous than his siblings. In contrast to Tom's sparkling, expressive blue eyes, Sam's were hazel and reposed nervously deep in his sockets. He had a habit of allowing his mouth to rest slightly but almost permanently open, which gave him the air of a boy who did not quite understand what was going on around him. He probably didn't. Sam did as he was told and there was a helplessness about him that pained Nell. His mother said he was a magnet for bad luck and was the sort of boy who would sneeze whilst standing behind the hind legs of an agitated horse. To make matters worse, he did spend time standing behind horses, not necessarily angry ones, when he and his pals would collect the manure deposited by working horses all over Battersea and Clapham for onward sale to the big house gardens at a penny a pail.

Some in the street said Sam was feeble-minded, but not in front of the family. If circumstances went against you, being 'feeble-minded' was a sufficient diagnosis to be carted off to one of the giant red-brick asylums on the outskirts of London.

Even as a boy, Sam possessed those large, sunken eyes which, coupled with his slight frame and lethargic posture, gave him the air of a starving child. Annie and Nell did everything they could to feed him up because of this. His frailty had left him very dependent on Nell and although she cared for the boy deeply, she worried about how he was going to cope as he grew older, and often she shooed him outside to play with the other boys. At first he did not like this because he was teased about holding his sister's hand, his propensity to cry and his dislike of football and games, but he eventually became part of the gang, even if they did dub him 'Sam, Sam, the horse-shit man'.

Teddy was a clever boy. His reading and writing skills had overtaken Sam's by the time he was six, and the teacher told Nell and his mother that he was a gifted child. It was the greatest compliment that had been paid to a Bradshaw pupil and made mother and daughter extremely proud. ''E's gifted, you know. That's what 'is school says. Proplee gifted,' Annie would tell all and sundry. At the same time, he was quiet and what people these days might call 'withdrawn'. He, too, preferred staying indoors with his mother and sister rather than playing out in the street and would sit for long periods cross-legged staring at the wall, very much in his own world.

'That boy likes 'is own company too much for 'is own good. That's 'is problem,' Annie would say to Nell, as Teddy sat motionless in front of them, oblivious that he was the topic of their conversation. When he did occasionally venture out, he'd set off in the morning alone and wouldn't be seen until dusk. He would easily lose a day, wandering around the free museums, galleries and parks of London.

Henry, or 'Baby 'Enry' as he was referred to long after he had clambered out of his pram, was an affectionate boy and full of energy. He enjoyed all the privileges of being the baby in a large family. Nell had doted on him since the day she kept the water coming for Mrs Davis – ''er from next door' – when she had delivered him for Annie one hot Sunday afternoon when Edward was happily drinking in the Mason's Arms, his Sunday lunchtime pub, despite knowing his wife was 'soon'. Mrs Davis had tugged Henry, slimy and bloody, from between his mother's legs and plopped him straight into Nell's arms as she attended to the mess below her. It took her mother several days to recover from the birth and Nell tended to the baby in every way she physically could. Nothing was ever said and it was not a problem between mother and daughter, but there was no doubt that Henry was Nell's baby as much as he was her mother's.

One lazy Saturday afternoon, brother Sam, who was then 13, took Henry out with his pals. 'Look after him, Sam,' yelled Nell, as she fed wet clothes through the mangle. She would not normally have let Sam take the boy out on his own, as the older brother had little sense of time and danger, but she was reassured because he was with the boys from the street. Urchins they were but streetwise and decent with it.

Once before, Sam had taken Henry out when Henry could not have been more than four years old. They had slipped off early in the morning and when they had not returned by nightfall panic had set in. Annie fetched a policeman, but he said there was nothing he could do, not knowing where to start looking. When they finally arrived home, not long before the clock showed 10, Annie went for Sam with the broom.

'Mum,' he pleaded, as he tried to ward off her blows, 'I was only showin' Baby 'Enry London town. We been on every tram going, Mum, and paid no more than a penny.'

'I bet you bloody 'ave!'

Nell was angry with Sam too, but her heart melted when she saw the injured look on his face and the tears well up in those sorrowful eyes. It was 1906, as Sam sauntered down Sleaford Street with Henry skipping after him, a year Nell could not forget, however foggy her mind became. It was August and the newspaper that Nell had read had reported that the previous day had been the hottest in years. As she worked her way through the laundry, the sweat trickled down her arms and legs. She knew she could not expect the boys to stay indoors on a day like that.

Sam returned home later that afternoon, with a policeman, and there was no sign of Henry. He was wailing and his body shook uncontrollably, as if possessed by some spirit. Nell knew instantly that something very, very terrible had happened.

It emerged that the boys had travelled up the river as far as Blackfriars Bridge, under the gaze of St Paul's Cathedral, mudlarking along the banks as they often did. Here, there was a small beach where all manner of debris was washed up and deposited as the tide retreated, and the boys picked through it believing, or hoping, they would find something they could sell. This was a popular pastime for children of the river: sometimes they did pick up a sealed crate that had fallen off one of the barges and contained something of use or value but, in truth, very rarely. Other people's rubbish would have been filtered for anything of value at least once before on its journey from house to river. Some of the older boys had waded into the water up to their waists as they pulled on some old rope, which they imagined had something on the end, but the cord kept coming and coming. Henry was in among them, splashing excitedly, and Sam remembers shouting at him to get back onto the beach as the water was up to his shoulders and neck. Henry thrashed around, keeping himself upright and afloat by standing and swimming as the sodden golden twine kept coming and coming and the excitement built.

'I reckon there's a body on the end of this bastard,' shouted Harry Love.

'It could be treasure,' bubbled Sam.

They did not notice the current that casually, and suddenly, sucked Henry from them, and carried him towards the middle of the river, until he shouted. 'Sam, Sam, help me!'

They did not panic at first, but then the speed with which he was being drawn from them increased. As if a deadly conspiracy was under way, another current came from nowhere and picked up the boy and tossed him out river as far as the first gigantic supporting pillar of Blackfriars Bridge. Henry tried to hug the huge concrete structure, but there was nothing to grip and he quickly slipped off. He tried again, like a tiny limpet clinging for life. Sam and the boys from Sleaford Street were now terrified, shouting and crying for help, but none swam out as far as the pillar, which Henry kept kicking and thrashing back to in forlorn attempts to clamber on top. But there were absolutely no footholds or handholds on the rotund, smooth construction. Within minutes, but what seemed an age to the tortured onlookers, who now included some helpless observers looking down from the bridge, Henry stopped struggling and allowed the power of the current to carry him down river. He was still alive minutes later when a man from a passing boat managed to pluck him from the water, but he had swallowed huge amounts of filthy Thames sludge and was unconscious. He died two days later in St Thomas' Hospital.

Henry's drowning devastated the Bradshaw family. Its repercussions would be felt for many years and even those who were not alive when it happened would carry the grief forward. Nell would tell her sons about Baby 'Enry and his drownin' and only with her passing would time render it painless. An invisible and intangible ghost of blame followed the Bradshaws everywhere and although this feeling was never discussed everyone carried it like a dull ache for the rest of their lives, unwittingly passing it down the generations. Edward blamed himself. If he had been bringing in more money, Annie would not have needed to work and she'd have been minding the children. He should have taught the boy to be a strong swimmer. After all, a lighterman's son, of all people, should be able to swim well. He took solace in even more drink. His wife felt she should have been there for her boy in his need. She could not bear to ask Sam if Henry had cried out for her because she knew that he would have done. She should have laid down rules for Nell about letting him out and Sam taking him. She blamed herself, she blamed Nell a little, she blamed Sam, but most of all she blamed Edward. Once young Henry was buried, she resolved to leave him.

Nell *knew* the blame rested with her, despite her mother's reassurances to the contrary. She should not have let Sam go off with Henry, especially after the last time, when they went on every tram in London. She should have asked where they were going. She should have kissed her baby brother goodbye. He'd been so keen to go out with Sam and his pals they had not even said cheerio to one another. She could not get the image of Henry skipping excitedly along in front of his slower, older brother out of her mind as he left the house for the last time, and neither could she remove the imagined but even more vivid pictures of his drowning and his panic and pain.

Sam retreated into himself and some say he died too that hot Saturday afternoon. Soon, it became the family way not to talk about Henry and his sad fate, especially in front of Sam, who believed that everyone blamed him for his little brother's death. What haunted Sam, he once told Nell in tears, was little Henry's small arms trying to embrace the pillar, to find a grip, and his look of terror when he could not. The image haunted Nell ever after, as did the terrible guilt and grief that poured out from Sam that day, when they were both adults and were sharing a Guinness when Sam had come to her one morning on his way home from the labour exchange. It was the first time they had spoken about Henry in 20 years. Sam was in the habit, then, of dropping in on Nell on his way home from his normally unsuccessful visit to the labour exchange and he would drink tea and smoke cigarettes whilst Nell busied herself around him. He sat in the chair not taking off his army greatcoat or cap and scarf as always. Usually, they exchanged small talk and avoided potentially upsetting topics like Sam's hopeless unemployment, Maggs's choice in men, their father and so on. This day, though, Nell had a large bottle of Guinness, which Tom had left the previous night, and they decided to share it. Whether it was the alcohol – Sam's emaciated body was no longer used to it – or not, Nell could not say, but he soon became very melancholic and started to talk about the day of Henry's drowning. 'I should have swum out to him, Nell.'

'It all 'appened so quickly; it's easy to say these things afterwards.'

'But it didn't 'appen quickly, Nell. That's the thing. It took ages. Poor kid kept getting to the pillar and then getting swept away, and then 'e got back there. Somehow. Baby 'Enry must have thought, why wasn't I swimming to him? He must 'ave thought that.'

'Harry Love was there and his brother and Tommy Pocock. They were all older and bigger than you. Better swimmers. They never swam out to 'Enry.'

'They weren't 'Enry's brother, were they?'

Brother's and sister's eyes met, an uncomfortable truth hanging almost visibly between them.

More than 30 years after the tragedy, during the Second World War, when Nell cleaned offices in Fleet Street, she would walk out onto Blackfriars Bridge on her way in to work. It was always very early and the first buses, cars and trams of daylight were rattling over the bridge. The occasional cormorant skimmed the water, flying with purpose upriver. She would stop awhile and look over at the stony beach where her two brothers had played and then at those uncompromising bridge supports and curse them for not having one little ridge or foothold for poor Henry to cling to. Without fail, she would pull the handkerchief from her sleeve and wipe tears from her eyes before composing herself again for a morning's charring.

VI

Moonlight Flit

Henry Knight was a good sort. Nell had known him since she was a small child. The Knights lived mainly in Wadhurst Road, Sleaford Street and Patmore Street, and William Knight, Henry's father, was also a lighterman and he and Edward Bradshaw knew each other well. The Knights also had the river in their blood, Henry's grandfather, Joseph, having been a waterman before the rapid building of bridges across the Thames had deprived him of his livelihood: no longer was there business in picking up passengers from the riverside steps and taking them to the other side. The Knights had four surviving children and Henry was somewhere in the middle. Although neither Nell nor Henry ever showed any romantic interest in one another, they always spoke when they met in the street, which was frequently. Henry had also been friendly with brother Tom for a while and would always enquire after his well-being.

'How's your Tom doing, Nell?' he said one day, as they both

waited for a tram outside the steam laundry on Battersea Park Road.

'I wish I knew, 'Enry. We 'aven't 'ad as much as a whisper from 'im in a year. 'E's been to Souf Wales, Souf America, Souf everywhere.'

'Last time he was back, I had a drink with him and he said he would write.'

''E'd say anything but his prayers, that one.'

Brother Tom had indeed traversed the world in the relatively short time since he left home. He stopped off at countries and then moved on again, as if he was taking that train across southern England and jumping out at the stations to convince himself he had actually been to a place. He did get to Wales and he did work down the coal mine but soon found it was not to his taste. A postcard to the family suggested it was the people rather than the arduous work that had prompted him to move on so quickly. What the Welsh postmaster must have thought when he processed Tom's card can only be imagined; it read, 'Moving on any day now. The Welsh people bellyache all day long and I can't stand any more.' Cards duly arrived from several European countries and then from more obscure lands. The last letter or card Nell could remember receiving was from Peru – a place she had barely heard of. Tom said he was mining tin.

Nell thought Henry a little strange, or at least different from the other young men of the area. For a start, most chaps of his age were already spliced and raising children. He didn't use the pubs really and you'd certainly never hear him singing along the road on a Friday night after they had chucked out. She liked the way he kept himself smart and his shoes highly polished. He was a natty dresser with clean hands and clipped and clean fingernails. He spoke well, almost posh. If you didn't know better, you would be forgiven for thinking he could have hailed from the other side of the river. Henry had chosen not to follow his father under oars, or his brothers into the railway yards, and had instead taken employment as a shop assistant in Arding & Hobbs (in an effort to give the shop its 'correct' name, Nell always erroneously referred to it as Harding & Obbs), the big department store down by Clapham Junction. If he did well for himself, it could one day lead to him managing his own department. He currently worked in menswear. That career path alone marked him out from most of the Battersea boys and led to a great deal of teasing about his sexuality and keenness for measuring inside legs. Henry took this all in his stride. He had a happy, easygoing outlook. For his part, Henry thought Nell a little strange too, or at least different from the other young ladies of the area. She had an air and a determination about her and in their brief conversations she revealed intelligence and a down-to-earth cynicism about everyday life that appealed to him. She was old beyond her years and never resorted to giggling, flirting or any affectations whatsoever in the company of boys. The way she made the best of her appearance and kept herself smart pleased him.

It was almost a year to the day after Baby Henry's drowning that Annie made her and Nell cocoa one evening after the younger children had been put to bed and invited her outside in the yard for a smoke. Mother and daughter often shared a non-tipped Weights – 'Arry Tates, they called them, after the popular music-hall star – before they turned in for the night.

'I'm leaving the drunken bastard on Friday,' Annie announced.

'Friday?' Nell could think of nothing better to say.

'Yes, Friday. I've arranged rooms on a road off Lavender Hill. When 'e goes to the pub on Friday, as soon as 'e goes, we do a flit.'

'All of us?'

'Why, do you wanna stay with 'is nibs?'

'No, course not.'

Annie straightened up, popped her cigarette packet back into her apron pocket and walked back indoors. That was that.

Nell went to bed with dread and sadness gripping her like a suffocating corset. She understood why her mother was doing what she was doing and she knew beyond doubt that she *would* do it and that she, Maggs, Sam and Teddy would all be going with her, but it pained her enormously. She could never forgive her father for delivering the blow that lifted her mother's feet from the ground and she cursed him for his drinking, but she still loved him. She understood a little bit more now about sex and men's desires and she could guess how difficult it was to cope with her father when he was feeling rampant in drink. If she were her mother, she'd do the same. She'd have done it long ago probably. But Edward was her daddy. Her old man. He was big and strong. She was his first surviving daughter and, as such, had had the privilege of cuddling into his lap when he relaxed in his chair after work when she was small. He did some bad things to Annie, but he was not a bad man; she couldn't say he was a bad man. Sometimes husbands struck their wives in drink – Bert Leverett pinned his wife's arm to the wall with a toasting fork during a row and she nearly died from poisoning of the blood, but nobody thought of him as evil personified and Gertie never left him. Nell ached inside as she imagined how her father was going to feel when he realised his entire family had walked out on him.

Those five days between Monday and Friday were among the worst of Nell's life because her father sat at the table eating his dinner, chatted, cleaned his shoes, went and came from the pub, and he had no idea that his life was about to change dramatically for the worse and for ever. Knowing that, while he was ignorant to it all, felt like a betrayal of the worst kind for Nell.

'What's wrong with you, gel?' he enquired of her on the

Thursday evening. Her stomach turned. She worried he would guess.

'Nuffin' wrong with me, Dad,' she lied.

'You've got a face like a month of bloody Sundays. Are you lovesick, gel?'

She wanted to cry and had the urge to throw her arms around her father and tell him everything and ask him to change his ways, but knew she could not, that he would not. It was a dangerous moment as her concerned father's eyes searched hers.

'Lovesick? She ain't even got a young man,' piped up Maggs, which led to admonishment from Edward over his younger daughter's flirtatious ways, and Nell went to fetch some coal for the fire.

Ironically, Edward went to work on the dreaded Friday and arrived home flushed with the river air rather than through drink. He sat on his chair at the table and Annie brought him his pewter of water and a bowl of bubbling hot stew. 'Come on, gel,' he said between chewing his meat and gristle, 'what's been 'appening in the world today, then?'

Nell picked up the newspaper and read the story from the front page, which was about women and police fighting outside the House of Commons. The women were incensed because they had delivered a petition to Prime Minister Henry Campbell-Bannerman, with hundreds of thousands of signatures, demanding that women be allowed to vote in political elections. Bizarrely, the PM had told the delegation that he agreed with their points but 'felt obliged to inform them he proposed to do nothing about it'. This did not go down well with the suffragettes.

It was customary for Edward to express his opinions on whatever story Nell relayed. 'I can't see what the problem is,' he commented that night. 'If the women want the vote, they should 'ave it. They 'ave to live 'ere as well.' Nell wished her father hadn't said that – if he had said that women were inferior and only good for cleaning and washing, it might have made what was going to happen in a couple of hours a smidgen easier.

Edward Bradshaw rose to his feet and changed from his work clothes into his suit and shirt. Nell wondered why he dressed up so on a Friday night: he went to the same pub as he did every other day of the week and drank and smoked with the same people. He then sat back down and polished his watch and then his shoes. He called Teddy over to him and took a penny from his waistcoat pocket, put it in his son's palm and folded his little hand around it. Annie stood by the washtub with her back to her husband and Nell busied herself with piles of laundry waiting to be ironed. Edward rubbed Teddy's hair and slipped out of the door without another word. They all heard him whistling as he passed the window. When Nell turned around, her eyes were full of tears and she pulled Teddy towards her and cuddled him, although the young boy could have had no idea that he would never live with his father again. Meanwhile, Annie continued to prod the washing with her wooden tongs until she was sure that her husband was safely ensconced in the saloon bar of the Duke of York.

'Go and fetch Maggs, and where's Sam, the daft ha'p'orth?' she barked. Maggs was next door; Sam was not home from work. Annie parked up two borrowed prams outside the front door and furiously started to pile in clothes, ornaments, photographs and food. She knew exactly what she was taking and what she was leaving. When Nell explained to Maggs what was happening, she promptly ran into the house to gather her few belongings. Teddy held Nell's hand nervously.

Sam, still little more than a boy himself, arrived home and stood with his hands on his hips. 'What's 'appening 'ere? We doing a moonlight flit?' he laughed. Moonlight flits were

commonplace in the locality. Entire families unable to pay their
rent and arrears to private landlords would pile their belongings
into bags and disappear from their homes under cover of the night
to set up elsewhere with a new landlord, hoping their luck would
change. Nell explained again and the smile disappeared from her
brother's face.

'Thanks for letting me in on the secret,' he whispered, as he too
hurriedly gathered some belongings. Sam was never one for
confrontation of any kind. Nell pushed one pram and Sam the
other, and Annie led the way: only she knew exactly where they
were going. Neighbours, who had seen many a family decamp in
this manner, came into the street to watch.

'Don't yer worry, Mrs Bradshaw, we ain't seen nuffin'. Make the
bastards whistle for their money.'

'Where are you off to, Annie?' shouted Mrs Davis.

'To the seaside,' Annie answered flippantly, as they turned into
New Road. Nell thought that answer a bit unkind to a neighbour
who had helped deliver some of her children, but she and Maggs
could not stop themselves giggling as they broke into a trot. Not
so many yards away, Edward drained the glass of his first pint of
mild of the night and placed it on the bar with just enough force
to alert the landlord he was ready for his second.

Annie was calm and resolute as they unloaded their belongings
into three empty rooms in Eland Road.

'Won't Dad come and find us and jus' fetch us 'ome?' asked
Maggs.

''E won't even notice,' grunted Annie. 'And, anyway, this is yer
'ome now.'

Nell was not so sure and half expected Edward to turn up that
night and lead Annie home by the ear just as the policeman had
done to Tom that day after he had misbehaved in the park. But he
didn't. Nor did he appear the next day or the day after.

Life settled down into a new routine very quickly. With Annie and Nell as breadwinners, they were not so badly off. Annie was charring still and Nell had got a job at the Crosse & Blackwell pickle factory. Maggs had now assumed Nell's parental role. She was keeping an eye on Sam and young Teddy, although she and Sam were both old enough now to go to work and Sam did drift around running errands and earning a few shillings here and there.

Nell remembers this period as a very happy time. Her mother relaxed noticeably and her natural sense of humour came to the fore. She was a great observer of the people around her and had nicknames for everyone. When neighbours stopped at the front door to chat, she'd participate happily, but as soon as they were out of earshot she would turn around and say to one of the children, 'Daft old boot!' The man across the road, who happened to be portly, bald and wore glasses, was 'Mr Pickwick' and their new neighbour, Mrs White, was the 'Duchess of Lambeth'. Annie called her Duchess because, in her opinion, she thought she was above herself. Nell could never see this and thought Mrs White a nice old girl, who kept herself to herself. Maybe that was the problem. Being above one's self, or 'stuck up', was a common accusation levied against each other in Battersea. It was acceptable to have aspirations to better oneself and get on in life but achieving any of those aspirations moved you into new territory and it caused discomfort for others.

Although there may have been less money coming into the house, all of it was under Annie's control and the family's circumstances improved dramatically, as she had known they would.

The move was good for Sam, too, because it took him away from the boys he had been with when Henry died. It was a burden of horror they all carried and although they endeavoured not to discuss the events of that afternoon, it bound them together in an unspoken chain of grief and guilt. 'Up the hill', Sam made new friends, who generally knew nothing of the tragedy and had no preconceived impressions of his character. He started to run around with these new boys and managed to keep out of trouble. Until the Brown Dog riots, that was.

The common people of Battersea were mainly uninterested observers in the row (if they were aware of it at all) that was being waged in the newspapers and the courts between medical students and anti-vivisectionists over the death of a dog in clinical tests. On one corner of Battersea Park stood the Anti-Vivi, a hospital opposed to all forms of animal experimentation for the progression of medical science. Because of Battersea's historical connection with dogs and its reputation as a radical area within London, members of various anti-vivisection groups decided to erect a statue of the dead dog in its memory. It would stand on the newly constructed Latchmere Estate, an early experiment in council housing.

When the 'Brown Dog' was finally unveiled, London's medical students became increasingly incensed and began marching and demonstrating in London about the memorial and what it stood for. Indeed, under cover of night, the students crept into Battersea and attempted to smash the statue to the ground. To many, it seemed those belonging to the medical profession were determined to persecute the animal in death as they had in life. However, it was the inscription that the students really objected to:

> In memory of the brown terrier dog done to death in the University College in February 1903, after having endured vivisection extending over two months and having been handed from one vivisector to another till death came to his release.

Battersea people only became involved when police began to flood the area in anticipation of a violent invasion of medical students. Most of the locals did not harbour strong views about vivisection, or even animals, but the notion of gangs of well-heeled but militant trainee doctors coming into their area bent on destruction was an affront to their dignity. The memorial – a statue of the dog on top of a drinking fountain – was made use of by the local children, so who did these toffs think they were coming to knock down something that their community used?

One particular night, the expectation that the students were coming was very strong. More police than had been seen before were lining Battersea Park Road and mounted police stood guard on Battersea Bridge, Albert Bridge and Vauxhall Bridge. Demonstrators opposed to the students had come into the area and were making themselves seen and heard, waving placards and banners. Behind those interlopers, in the houses, alleys and shadows, almost every boy, young man and plenty of the women of Battersea were quietly prepared for trouble. In the backstreets, boys hung around in small groups, hands thrust in pockets, fingering catapults and sharpened stones; in the pubs, men had all come prepared, many carrying a fireside poker up their sleeves or in their belts, others clasping knuckledusters, and a few secreting knives. The women stood in their aprons on their doorsteps or in small groups, arms folded defiantly, their square-jawed stance daring the upstart students to come into their streets. It was a cold winter's night with a cocktail of fog and menace hanging heavily in the air.

The expected mass invasion did not materialise, the police in the centre of London managing to contain the bulk of the demonstrators, although small groups did manage to slip through the cordon and turn up in Battersea. They received a rude awakening, as they walked into the wrath of an angry community.

Sam Bradshaw was with a group of boys who received an urgent street message that a dozen students had arrived via Chelsea Bridge and were making their way down Prince of Wales Drive. They had broken into three groups to avoid immediate detection. Sam and his pals ran from the Latchmere Estate, up Battersea Park Road and cut through Macduff Road to intersect the students. As they approached the demonstrators, they pelted them with stones and mud but underestimated the students' willingness to fight. Sam found himself in a tussle with a well-built young man in his prime and took a fearful hiding from his fists before being rescued by a policeman, his only consolation being the sight of his assailant falling in a heap as the policeman's truncheon rained down on his head.

Sam was taken to the police station and booked, but because of his young age and the very visible evidence of the battering he had already received, he was not charged. Instead, an officer took him back to his new house in Eland Road.

'Sorry, missus, but young Samuel here has been fighting down at the Brown Dog fountain with all the mobs. As you can see, he's got the worse of it. I reckon you should keep him indoors till all this blows over.'

Annie delivered a swift punch to Sam's stomach. As he lurched forward with wind hissing out of his mouth, she pulled him in the door by his hair. 'Thank you, sir,' she said to the policeman as she shut the door.

The Brown Dog disturbances continued on and off for many months, although some of the worst rioting occurred in the centre of London. Sam kept well away from them, wherever they were; he'd gone off dogs. Huge amounts of money and police resources had been expended in guarding the statue and containing the demonstrators, and Battersea Council, who had given permission for the memorial and its inflammatory inscription in the first place, eventually instructed its workers to dismantle the statue in the dead of night.

Meanwhile Edward did discover his family's whereabouts and appeared on the doorstep a couple of times. The first occasion was early one evening two months after their night flight. Annie closed the door behind her and walked out into the street with him. Nell assumes she did this because her husband was less likely to become aggressive in daylight in full view of the entire street. They talked for over an hour, but not once did Annie alter her uncompromising body language, with legs slightly apart and arms folded.

''E asked when we were coming 'ome,' explained Annie when Edward had finally left peacefully and forlorn. 'I told 'im I was not coming 'ome ever, but you kids were free to do as you please. 'E gave me £5, which is more than I've 'ad out of 'im for years, and I give it back. We don't need 'is money. 'E had the drink on 'im and had the cheek to say it was 'genst the law us moving out. That's a new one on me. Give me strength. 'Genst the law. Can you credit it? He even said that if there were a man involved, he'd thrash the life from him. I says to 'im, "Anover man? You think I want anover man after you? Thank you, but no thank you." Can you credit it? I've 'ad enough of men for more than one lifetime, thank you very much. That's what I said to 'im, silly old fool.'

The second time Edward arrived at the door was the following year, and he was sober and dressed in his Sunday best: hat, waistcoat and all. Nell was shocked by his appearance, though, as he seemed to have shrunk. His shoulders, made broad by working the oars for years and years, had collapsed and he stooped slightly. His cheeks were the mottled red of alcohol-tinged skin, rather than the blooming red of the river wind, and seemed sucked in. His hair was now fully grey, although it was neatly combed. He was nearly 60 years old and was beginning to look it. This time, he asked to see the children and Annie reluctantly let him in. After all, it was a Sunday and the family were ready to go to church themselves. He stood awkwardly in the room, jingling the change in his pocket.

'Come on, Annie, this 'as gorn on long enough. Can't you all come on 'ome. I'm an old man now and can't be living on me own.'

'I told you before, Edward, I ain't coming 'ome. Not now, not never. If any of these children here want to go back, I'm not stopping them.'

Edward was a proud man and he must have been desperate to come round and plead like he did. Nell could see that, and the crushed and helpless look he gave Annie, then the kids, burnt into her heart. He had tried so hard to look so smart and be so calm and sober in an effort to reignite those feelings his wife once certainly had for him. But the involuntary shaking of his hands betrayed his body's need for beer and whisky. Nell felt so desperately sorry for him as he stood there a broken man. Sam and Maggs interrupted the awkward silence with sobs, whilst Teddy stared pointedly at the floor.

'Well, yoose all know where I am,' he said as he put his head down and walked out of the door. That was the last time any of them saw Edward Bradshaw.

VII

Little Big Man

Maggs liked the Clapham Junction end of Battersea far more than down by the river and the goods yards. There were bigger and better shops, more modern pubs, the music halls, the busy station and lots of new and interesting people. In her eyes, there was more going on. It wasn't Chelsea, but it certainly wasn't Sleaford Street, Wadhurst Road or Savona Street. The ground-floor rooms in Eland Road were spacious and there was even a little garden area at the front – landlords were snapping up these newly built houses and cramming two or more families into one house: for Maggs, it meant going up in the world. Just across Lavender Hill, posh houses were sweeping back to Clapham Common and professional families were moving in. Maggs could foresee an exciting new wave of interest from a new batch of local men. Annie and Nell felt differently. The Sleaford Street community had been their life for generations and knowing that in almost every other house lived a relative of some sort fostered a great sense of togetherness and although they were not even two miles up the road it could have been twenty.

It was in the Stanley Arms, almost directly across the road from their house, where Maggs first noticed Tichy Thorogood. The public house was situated on the corner of Lavender Gardens and Lavender Hill and soon became the family's pub of choice. Nell, Annie and Sam all popped in for a Guinness or a mild and Maggs used it as much as she could get away with. Annie did not like her daughter going in any pub without them, but Maggs was a hard one to control, especially after she got her job at Prices, the candle factory, and was earning her own keep.

It soon became apparent Tichy was not the type of man she imagined meeting up on Lavender Hill. He was not a young doctor or clerk. Tichy was a small man but incredibly thick-set and solid – that was the first thing that struck you about him. His thick clothes and overcoats seemed to accentuate his muscular frame. He wore a bowler hat and a dark-brown suit in nearly all weathers. He had a liking for jewellery, and a gold watch hung from his jacket and rings adorned his disproportionately large fingers. When they were wrapped around a pint of mild, the glass became an egg cup. When he arrived in the pub, the other men seemed to defer to him and Maggs noticed that sometimes he did not appear to pay for his drinks. She thought he was in his late 20s or early 30s and was immediately taken by his sharp dress sense and general aura. Someone told her when she asked that his name was Tichy and he was not a man to be messed with – Maggs made a mental note to mess with him.

One evening, as she and a work pal sat at a table after a hard day at the candle factory, she spied Tichy looking at her in the reflection of the big whisky mirror, as he stood at the bar. Eyes met and held. Without turning around or moving an inch, he mouthed 'I love you' at the mirror and her reflection, at which her mouth fell open in utter shock at his unashamed impudence. However, he carried on drinking, never said a word or turned around to face her, and a few minutes later he left the pub with another man without a second glance. It was a defining moment. Maggs was accustomed to the attentions of men and enjoyed playing them along, but now Tichy Thorogood became her obsession. Brother Sam was doing some running for a local street bookie and she asked him to find out some more about the small man with the big aura. The news was not good.

'Tichy Thorogood's 'is name. From the Elephant way. They say 'e can fight two men at a time and still come out on top, and 'e knows some bad people. Works with the Italians from Clerkenwell. Takes money from the bookies. Takes goods from the railways. Sells stuff. Cliff Gilbert says you should keep away from 'im if you 'ave any sense. 'E's been in prison before and Cliff thinks 'e's married.'

Maggs vowed to introduce herself formally next time he was in.

A fortnight later, she was in the Stanley with a group of girls and some of the men from Whiteway's cider factory. They were enjoying their early Friday evening because they had their pay packets safely zipped up in their pockets and felt temporarily rich. Tichy pushed open the saloon door, strolled in and stood up against the bar. He removed his hat and slipped off his elegant white gloves. The barman brought him a whisky and splashed in some soda. Maggs, fortified by beer, left her table and stood next to him, waiting to be served.

'Can I get you a drink, my darlin'?' he smiled.

'Yes, please, Tichy. I think I will. I'll have a sherry, if that's all right.'

'If it wasn't all right, Tichy wouldn't be asking, would 'e? And 'ow do you know my name is Tichy?'

'Someone told me.'

'So, you've been asking around who I am, 'ave you? Tichy got your 'eart fluttering, as 'e?'

'No, I just wondered who you were, that's all.'

'No need to be shy with Tichy. What's your name anyway? Because I noticed you, too. You're the prettiest thing this side of Stockwell, I can tell you that. Me and you need to be friends, that's what I say. What do you say?'

'Yes. I say yes. And the name is Margaret, but they call me Maggs.'

'Good show, Maggs. I like that. Maggs. Maggs and Tichy. Tichy and Maggs. Go together, don't they? Like Romeo and Juliet. Victoria and Albert. Jack and Jill. Gin and tonic. I think you'll 'ave to be Tichy's girl. What do you say?'

'Yes, I think I will,' sighed Maggs, falling helplessly under Tichy's spell.

'Yes, think you will what?'

'Yes, I'll have to be Tichy's girl.'

'Good. That's settled.'

Meanwhile, Nell continued to bump into Henry Knight on his way to and from work at Arding & Hobbs, and a familiar face from the Dogs Home end of Battersea was a welcome sight to her. He invited her to the Grand with him one evening and Nell accepted. It would be her first ever date. The Grand was the best of the local music halls. Annie would often urge Nell to go out, saying she would never meet a young man if she was tied to the house and the children and it was not fair. But Nell felt differently – she had no real interest in young men or walking out. She believed that she had to help her mother bring up the family: she still felt in a small but nagging way responsible for Henry's death and worried about Sam and young, introverted Teddy if she was not around watching them. Teddy was still a solitary child, who rarely wanted to play out with the other children, and was very attached to his mother and sisters. They thought that Baby Henry's death had affected him very badly, although he never mentioned it.

Maggs was fine, thought Nell. She could look after herself. At 16, she was already walking out with the keen young men of Battersea and even travelling up the road to Nine Elms to hobnob with the boys up there. Battersea people always felt that folk from Nine Elms were that little bit more rough; Nine Elms people felt the same about the Elephant boys and the Elephant boys were probably wary of the lads from Bermondsey way.

Maggs and Nell shared a love of the music hall and they managed to go along to the Grand every other weekend with their new friend, Mary Flynn, who lived next door on the other side to Mrs White. The Shakespeare Theatre, also a music hall, was almost on their doorstep, but it was the Grand, 'up the Junction', that attracted the best acts. They had seen them all over the years: Marie Lloyd, Dan Leno, Little Tich, George Formby senior, George Robey, Will Hay, Harry Lauder, Harry Tate, Vesta Tilley and the rest. Each and every one so special to their audience. Dan Leno himself had laid the foundation stone for the Clapham Grand and a bigger national hero you could not find. When he died, still a relatively young man, in 1904, there was an outbreak of public mourning not seen since the Queen had died. The music hall was such a wonderful experience, where everybody sang along with the performers and knew all the words. They laughed aloud with the good comedians and barracked loudly the bad ones, marvelled at the magicians and admired the beautiful dancers. Nell could never understand how the music halls lost out to cinemas. How could people enjoy moving photographs of the stars over the real thing? You could still shout out to Valentino or Charlie Chaplin, but they could not shout back. It always baffled her.

Marie Lloyd was the sisters' favourite. She was one of them: a girl from a rough part of London, trying to make the best of her life and keeping cheerful at all times. They knew the words to all her lyrics and sang along raucously to the choruses of 'My Old Man Said Follow the Van' and 'Oh, Mr Porter!', and her act 'I'm One of the Ruins that Cromwell Knocked About a Bit'. They delighted in her sauciness and knew that when she leant forward with an air of conspiracy and hissed 'Any *perlice* in?', she was about to impart a remark that some might think obscene. For the adoring audience in the Grand, the racier the better. Her private life was actually very public and the more problems Marie had with her jealous husband, her boyfriend jockey, who won the Epsom Derby, and the demon drink, the more the music-hall-going public empathised with her. Like Leno, Marie died prematurely; it was the liquor that inevitably killed her. Her death also provoked scenes of mass mourning. Working girls like Nell, Maggs and Mary Flynn felt like they had lost a friend.

Little Tich was another idol – a diminutive comedian who came onto the stage in a bowler hat and wore long shoes far too big for him. It was said he had five fingers and a thumb on each hand and also possessed more than the standard number of toes, but Nell and Maggs never got close enough to see. He and Marie were the biggest names in London for some years after Dan Leno died and it was while watching Little Tich one night from the cheap stalls that Maggs cottoned on to how 'Tichy' Thorogood had got his nickname.

Nell and Henry started going to the Grand together regularly. He began to knock for Nell on his way up from Wadhurst Road. Annie took to him straight away, as did Sam, Teddy and Maggs. They never asked if he had seen Edward down the river and he never volunteered any information about their father. He must have seen him, living only a couple of streets away. Nell thought him handsome, but although she enjoyed his company and felt good holding his arm as they set off down the hill, she did not feel she loved him in any way and the thought of kissing him had been dismissed early on. She disputed the notion that they were courting and Henry never tried to insist they were. He seemed to be as relaxed as her about conducting the relationship on this basis and that was what Nell liked most of all. She was not ready for any of that romance palaver.

When Maggs said that Tichy Thorogood was accompanying them to the Grand one weekend, Nell was not best pleased. ''E's older than me. 'E's older than 'Enry. 'E's 30, if he's a day. You're still a gel. What do Mum say?'

'Mum says nuffin' coz Mum don't know.'

Mum soon did, though, because that Friday night Tichy breezed into the house and smacked three packets of Black Cat cigarettes down on the drop-leaf table. 'These are for you, Mother.' He fished around in his overcoat pocket and threw another packet over to Sam.

'Does 'e smoke yet?' he asked, jerking his thumb at 14-year-old Teddy and chucking another packet in his direction. 'Don't worry, Mother. I'll bring her home safe and sound. Tichy's a proper gentleman, you'll soon learn that.' He smiled as he made a crook of his elbow for Maggs to slip her arm through. Nell and Henry raised their eyebrows and smiled as they followed the couple out of the door.

'And what does you do, 'Enry, old son, to make a crown?' enquired Tichy, as he called for drinks in the saloon bar of the Falcon, where they had stopped for a quick one before going inside the Grand.

'I work across the road there, in Arding & Hobbs,' replied Henry, pointing out of the window.

'Really?' Tichy's interest was quickly roused. 'D'you get clobber on the cheap?'

'No, not really.'

'If you 'ear of anyfing going cheap or going out the back door, let Tichy know, won't you, 'Enry? We could both do all right.'

''E won't do all right if he loses his bloomin' job,' Nell interrupted.

Tichy insisted on paying for all four of them at the box office and again for the drinks when the show had finished, and when they got back to the house he knelt down and kissed Maggs's hand before striding off up towards the Wandsworth Road. Maggs was dizzy with it all. Henry had noticed she had spent most of the time in the Grand watching Tichy and not the stage. Nell felt distinctly uneasy.

'When are you going to marry that poor man?' Annie would often ask her daughter about Henry Knight.

'I don't want to be married,' Nell would reply. Annie would never press it further because she couldn't pretend that her own marriage had been a good one. She did point out, though, that Henry would not wait for ever. Nell would shrug and say that was his look out. Henry seemed as happy with the status quo as Nell was. She wasn't going to ask him and if he wasn't going to ask her, then they probably would never be wed. At home, though, Teddy was now approaching the time when he could go to work and that would mean that Annie only needed to keep herself. The pressure would be off in terms of having to bring in enough money to bring up the family. Nell would be staying at home now because she wanted to, not because she had to.

Sam had now left Eland Road. Nell had started working with a young girl named May Davis at the Crosse & Blackwell factory and she had taken her down to the Stanley one day after work. May was a quiet girl, with very striking looks, and brother Sam was immediately smitten by her. It was the first time Sam had shown an interest in a girl that Nell knew about and she was pleased when he and May started courting. She still worried about Sam and hoped for a good woman to take care of him. He remained physically weak and, in her opinion, too eager to please; others were apt to take advantage of him. Nell had torn a strip off the coal merchant when she discovered he was paying Sam a boy's wage when he was humping sacks of coal for him all day. Sam would never have said a word. May was soon pregnant, so a marriage was hastily arranged and a house found on the new Latchmere Estate.

The wedding reception in 1911 was held in a private room in the Latchmere public house. Sam had suggested inviting his father, but Annie had said that if he came she would not. Sam was not one to make a stand. Although Edward would surely have heard that his son was getting married, he never showed up or attempted to make contact with Sam. Nell remembers the party well because it was the first time all of the family, save Edward, had been together for a while and it would also be the last. A regular from the pub kindly joined them and played the piano as they sang along to their favourite music-hall songs. Bill was there with Dolly and their older children, and even Tom was back from the Peruvian silver-nitrate mines, where he had been working. Maggs was showing off Tichy, who smoked a large cigar and wore a loud checked suit, and Henry discreetly accompanied Nell. She treasured a photograph which survived from that day for the rest of her life. It still stood on her mantelpiece at Mysore Road in the 1980s, having survived all manner of domestic upheavals, including German bombs. Bill stands at one end with his arm around an impossibly young and nervous-looking Sam. They could easily have been father and son. Sam doesn't look old enough to run an errand to the shops let alone get wed. Tom is next and even in faded black and white it can be seen that his complexion is far darker than everyone else's from a few years of living in warmer climates. A cigarette hangs perilously from the side of his mouth. Beside him is Henry, wearing a shy smile, thinking perhaps he should not be in the photograph. Nell, Annie and Teddy form the front row and Maggs stands slightly apart from the group on the far right. The picture has been carefully cropped with scissors almost taking off Maggs's left arm, but if you look carefully you can see a hand curling around her waist. The hand is bejewelled and the fingers resemble Harris pork sausages. It belongs to Tichy Thorogood. Nell has been particular but not completely thorough in removing him from the family history.

VIII

Hops, Hits and Kisses

It was her eldest son Bill who came round to see Annie and told her that Edward, her estranged husband, had voluntarily entered the workhouse at Tooting Graveney. It sent a shiver down their spines. He was 62 years of age and had confided in nobody that he could not pay the rent on his house in Sleaford Street and had no means of support. Bill had called round to see him and found that another family were already living in their old home. Bill traced him to the Union Workhouse and went to see his father.

'Mum, 'e's a broken man,' he said. 'They sit there in rows all facing ahead, the poor wretches. Nobody speaking. 'E don't belong in that hellhole, do 'e?'

''E's not my child and 'e's not my 'usband and 'as not been for nearly seven years now.'

'Someone must take him in. We can't leave 'im to rot in the workhouse. I would meself 'ave 'im but with five sprogs and one on the way it ain't possible.'

'Who can take 'im? Sam an' May don't 'ave enuff room to swing a cat and 'e ain't coming 'ere. Even if I wanted it. We don't 'ave the room.'

Annie was not to be moved. They did have the room; Nell knew it and so did Annie. When Bill left after urging his mother to at least go and visit the old man, she and Nell sat silently with their thoughts. The irony of the events of a quarter of a century earlier, when Annie had persuaded Edward to take his father in and prevent him from ending his days in the workhouse, was not lost on them.

Even Nell thought that her mother's refusal to take Edward in was too harsh. Surely the Bradshaws would not let one of their own perish in the workhouse? Families stuck together against whatever life threw at them and only people without relatives ended up there. She knew what sort of life her father must have been living. If he was considered reasonably fit, they'd have him performing some sort of menial work. Daily life was run to a strict schedule of rising, working, eating and sleeping. There was no variation, and males and females were segregated – even married couples who had shared a bed for 30 years. The only real difference between the workhouse and a prison was theoretically you could walk out at any time. But, of course, you couldn't. The total lack of alternatives saw to that.

Annie, as always, knew what her daughter was thinking. 'I can't 'ave 'im back, dear. I really can't. You don't know the 'alf of it, you really don't. And I ain't never going to tell you.'

Nell always wondered what her mother meant by this, as she said it often enough afterwards. She could only imagine that the blow she witnessed her father delivering that evening was not the only one. Perhaps she endured more under the blankets than Nell could have known. Still, she felt that she was old enough and close enough to her mother to be taken fully into her confidence, and the fact she would never say more was the only thing she ever held against Annie. It was not fair to imply some terrible thing and expect her daughter to feel equally strongly but not tell her what it was.

Another thing Annie often said annoyed all of the family, not just Nell. She would declare, 'I will put up with most oaths, blasphemies and curses in my house, but there is one word that will not be uttered. If it is, whoever speaks it will be turned out on the street.'

'What word is that then, Mum?'

'Well, I can't say it, can I? Never 'ave, never will,' answered Annie.

'Well, 'ow can we know what it is?'

'You'll know all about it if you say it.'

None of the children ever discovered what the word was that enraged their mother so, although they all had their suspicions; but curiously Nell upheld the tradition with her children and they with theirs, slavishly banning the word for the next century, although nobody could be quite certain what it was.

If Nell and Maggs's first love was the music hall, Annie's was the annual hopping 'holiday' the whole family endeavoured to take each summer. Of course, it was a holiday in perception only; indeed, most of the Londoners who descended on the hop farms of Kent each year toiled harder picking the hops than they did at home in their factories and yards. Annie loved the anticipation: the trip up to London Bridge, the boarding of the special trains and the raucous journey down, then being disgorged by the hundred at the railway station in the tiny Kent village of Headcorn, where the Bradshaws and many of the old Sleaford Streeters came year in, year out. Their parents and grandparents had worked the same farms. It was like a curtain had been raised. Although they were barely 20 miles out of London, she and her family had entered a different world: a place where the locals 'talked funny', where the predominant colour was green not grey or brick-red, and exotic animals, like rabbits and hares, ran startled through the hop alleys. The air tasted noticeably better and the rivers only had ducks and swans floating on them rather than barges full of coal, timber and bricks. Annie relished the camaraderie, as families set down together in barns and huts, fighting for their own space and recreating as best they could their rooms at home. Whilst Annie brought precious little in the way of clothes, she always packed a few familiar ornaments and some blankets from their own beds.

They worked together as a family, taking their bins full of the picked hops to be measured by the tallyman and have their cards marked. At the end of the week when the farmer paid them, they normally had a good amount of money to take home to Battersea. They could do this only because there were no men in their party subbing their combined wages from the farmer to finance heavy drinking each night. Most people went home empty-handed but having had a lively and eventful time. Nell enjoyed it too but was disapproving of the loosening of morals that she sometimes witnessed when the drink had been flowing and the revellers of both sexes crammed into unlit huts for the night and lay down on their beds stuffed with faggots, the bundles of sticks left by the farmers so the hoppers could make their beds. Nell was always one to guard her privacy and was careful with which families the Bradshaws shared accommodation. She was positive, in the pitch-black and under the haze of drink, that some people could not be sure with whom they were canoodling, and when babies were born the following year she wondered if some mothers really knew who the fathers were.

It was whilst down hopping in 1913 that Nell and Henry shared their first long and tender kiss. It had taken over three years for the relationship to move to this stage. It was the last night of the trip, and everyone had been weighed on and was out in force in the village before the journey home in the morning. Headcorn had one long, wide high street that supported several pubs, and Nell and Henry left the last one to head back to the farm, cutting through the old graveyard on the way. They walked arm in arm, as always comfortable with one another. Behind the church itself, they drifted into an embrace and the kiss ensued. She enjoyed it, even though tobacco mixed with stout was the dominant taste. They stayed in the churchyard for some minutes exploring this new sensation, and then parted mouths and said no more as they walked to their hut. Henry stumbled up to the far end, where the men were kipping down, and Nell lay on her straw bed next to her mother and Teddy. Both lay awake for a while unable to ignore the stifled grunts, giggles and gasps of those who had less self-control than they.

A favourite hopping story passed down the generations was the tragic case of poor Nellie Suttie, a cousin of the Bradshaws. Nellie was the daughter of one of Annie's younger sisters, who lived down Sheepcote Lane in Battersea. Although she was a cousin of Nell's, they did not know each other well, her parents being a lot younger than Annie and having moved further down Battersea Park Road towards Wandsworth. Nell was a working-class snob if ever there was one and, for her, people from Sheepcote Lane were a step down the social ladder – family or no family. The houses were falling down even when she was young and the poverty was more marked than in the Dogs Home area. Gypsy caravans had been parked up for years at the bottom of the lane and the two communities had gradually interbred, forming a tough race of swarthy individuals quick with their tempers and their fists. There was one large family called Hurn, which boasted more than 12 brothers. With the beer inside them, they would fight like dogs, drawing blood and breaking bones only to be the best of friends the following day. Nell remembers when her husband was in Millbank Hospital, Old Man Hurn was two or three beds down, coughing his guts up with emphysema. One evening, his wife and daughter marched up to his bed and without further ado the wife punched the patient, her husband, full on in the face with her powerful fists. 'Leave 'im, Mum, 'e's dying,' the daughter remonstrated, but the mother proceeded to try to drag her wasted husband out of the bed. Nell never found out what heinous crime he had committed on his wife, but she was certainly not going to allow the man to die quietly.

Nellie Suttie was a very pretty girl; you could not help noticing her when you were down hopping. The boys would not take their eyes off her and a small army of besotted teenagers jostled with one another to work the alleys alongside her. One fateful afternoon, she took poorly and had to be carried back to her hut, where she was laid down on her bed and covered with an old blanket. When someone looked in on her only half an hour later, she was lifeless and cold. A doctor was called and pronounced her dead, saying that she had suffered a heart attack. How he could tell, nobody was sure. It seemed an unlikely cause of death for someone so young and apparently healthy. Work was stopped and Nellie was laid out in the farmer's house, where respects were paid all afternoon and evening. The family could not afford to take the body home for a funeral, so the vibrant teenager was buried the next day in the hop fields, with the local vicar carrying out the impromptu ceremony. A small stone was erected to mark the spot. Each year, until the 1950s, when there was nobody left going hopping who remembered the pretty, vivacious young girl, those who knew Nellie Suttie would come to lay and tend flowers.

Maggs had already stopped hopping by the time Nellie died. Only a couple of years earlier, she had been crowned Queen of the

Hops by the other Londoners and never had she revelled so much in being the centre of attention. But Tichy had started to control her at this stage and going down hopping was beneath her, he said. In reality, he was jealous. He did not like her to be around other men when she was not on his arm. As her mother and sister constantly told her, the relationship was not a healthy one.

He had been married, he had confessed, to his childhood sweetheart from the Elephant and Castle, but they were now estranged, awaiting divorce. There were no children from the marriage, he claimed – though everyone but Maggs doubted this. He only appeared in Battersea at weekends and was vague about what he did for a living and even where he actually lived. He sometimes called himself a 'buyer' and at other times a 'salesman'. It was obvious to everyone, again except Maggs, that he traded in stolen goods, among other things. When Annie and Nell discovered that Maggs had spent the night with Tichy at a hostel in Tooley Street in Bermondsey, their attitudes hardened. 'If you're laying down with that man, gel, 'e must marry you,' her mother demanded.

''E will,' retorted Maggs.

''E can't,' Nell reminded them both, ''e's already wed. Mum's right, Maggs, you'll find yourself in trouble and Tichy won't be there when you do. Mark my words.'

''E's not a good man. 'Is eyes near on touch,' proclaimed Annie.

''E's always been good to me, a real gentleman. And I don't do nuffin' I don't want to and 'e's got lovely eyes.'

'Find yerself a young man, gel. A boy yer own age. You don't want to be visiting the gaol when you're carrying 'is child. Cos that's what I see, I do.'

Tichy picked up quickly on the family's gathering disapproval of his relationship with Maggs, but he did not care. They'd been together four years now, and Maggs was a woman of twenty and able to make her own decisions. His lifestyle had not altered: he spent weekends in and around Battersea and weekdays elsewhere. Whilst he seemed devoted to and genuinely fond of Maggs there was no mention of marriage or how his divorce was progressing. Maggs was afraid to ask, but after the accumulation of much pressure from Annie and Nell she began to question Tichy over where the relationship was going. He did not take kindly to such probing.

'You ain't come of age yet, Maggs,' he told her. 'You're still a young girl. Tichy don't want people saying he took advantage of you, does he now? And divorces take time. I can't marry you just like that. What's the matter with you? I've not got eyes for anyone else, 'ave I? I've got enough on my plate without you in my ear'ole all day long.'

Maggs would then stop asking. She didn't like upsetting Tichy.

Nell was less reticent and on Empire Day 1913 her relationship, such as it was, with Tichy Thorogood came to an explosive end. The pubs had extended opening hours for the holiday and the factories had shut down. Union flags and bunting hung from shops and houses. The people of Battersea were marking the occasion in the drinking dens of the area, many of them standing outside in the warming sun. Nell and Henry, Mary Flynn and her new husband, and one of Henry's brothers had gone down to the Latchmere public house to share some drinks with Sam and May. The young couple were now also parents to their first child, May, and Sam had found his first regular work as a cleaner and general helper at the large Morgan Crucible works. Nell was so pleased for him, and Sam was so proud to be standing on his own two feet, supporting a wife and family. Meeting May had been the making of him.

Maggs and Tichy arrived in the early evening, having taken a drive in a friend's motor car in the Oxfordshire countryside, where Tichy had connections. She was the first Bradshaw to sit in a motorised vehicle and she spent an hour talking about this new experience. Tichy was on top form and was nattily dressed in his check suit and bowler hat, with his customary white gloves and the added touch of a white silk handkerchief in his breast pocket. Both had already drunk a fair bit and showed no sign of abating after their arrival at the Latchmere. Maggs made the mistake of smiling and returning conversation to a young man of her own age, which Tichy noticed. He whispered some words to the boy and he quickly fled the pub with the look of a frightened rabbit. He then took Maggs to one side. When they returned to the group, she was suitably chastened. Noticing the change in her younger sister's demeanour but not realising what had taken place, Nell called out to her over the general babble of drink-fuelled conversation.

'What's come over you, Maggs? You feeling queer?'

'No, I'm fine, Nell.'

'You gorn a bit quiet, gel.'

'She was making plenty of noise last night, I can tell you,' interjected Tichy, 'when she was crawling all over me in the pit. You 'ad the devil in you last night, didn't you, gel?'

As he laughed aloud at his own crudity, the group fell quiet. Maggs looked at the floor, her curls falling onto her face, covering her embarrassment. Sam tried to plug the silence and asked who wanted a drink, but Nell literally flashed red. She pushed Henry and Sam aside and smashed Tichy under the jaw with an uppercut that would have done Jem Mace proud.

It was a good hit. No doubt. One that was talked about in the Latchmere for many years after. It lifted the little man off his feet, but it did not put him down. He raised his gloved hand to his chin, stroking it as if not believing he had been struck, as Nell berated him. 'You do not talk about my sister like that. Go back to the Elephant or wherever it is you come from. You're not wanted down 'ere.'

Carefully, and ominously, he took off his gloves and laid them on the bar. He did not reply to Nell as he removed his jacket and handed it to a stranger standing behind him. 'Shut your cake'ole, you fat fucking cow,' he spat suddenly. 'You shouldn't have done that because you know Tichy can't strike a woman, don't you? So, I'm sorry, but it's your own fault.'

At that, he swung around and crushed his mallet-like fist into Sam's unsuspecting and innocent face, bursting his nose in the process.

IX

The War and the Workhouse

Poor Sam's nose never looked the same again. He was a living and walking reminder of how Tichy Thorogood had cursed the Bradshaw family. It was a bad time for all concerned, and Annie was furious with Nell for causing Tichy to strike innocent Sam as he had. Sam, as always, took the incident in his stride; it was almost as if he felt life was supposed to deal him terrible blows, both physical and emotional, but the repercussions rippled for some time.

Annie demanded Maggs sever all connections with Tichy and this she did – for a while. Her blind love for him came to the fore again and after a month or two, when she was seen with Tichy in a pub on the Wandsworth Road one evening by a family friend, Annie asked her to leave home.

Strangely – or not so strangely – Maggs did not move in with Tichy, the man she had been courting for nearly five years, but instead went to live with the family of a workmate in Silverthorne

Road. She did still come to see her family in Eland Road and they never stopped talking to each other. The subject of Tichy was taboo at home: nobody asked and Maggs did not volunteer information about what was happening in their lives. When others saw Tichy, he was openly hostile; until the war broke out it could be very unpleasant for any of the Bradshaws if they bumped into him in any of the pubs around Lavender Hill. He was particularly rude to Henry one day when they had passed in the street, suggesting Henry was a dandy and a 'nancy boy', and ending by saying smarmily, 'Give Tichy's love to Nell, won't you.' Once the war had started, there were far more important things to worry about – for everyone.

The war had begun without almost anyone in the Bradshaw household noticing. They still took the newspaper and Nell still read to the family, although Teddy could read far better than his sister by now. She preferred to focus on the detail of the grisly murders that the newspapers delighted in reporting rather than political upheavals in the far corners of Europe. One case they had all salivated over a couple of years earlier was the murder on Clapham Common of an Eastern European man and the subsequent arrest and trial of another European called Steinie Morrison. Steinie had lived a few yards from their house for a while above the baker's shop on Lavender Hill and although the family did not know him, they knew the couple that owned the baker's well. They said Steinie was a decent man and that they could not believe he was a murderer. The case was made all the more real to Nell and Teddy because they walked out on the common a day or two after the murder and surveyed the flattened grass where the body had lain. The murder had come soon after the Sidney Street Siege, in which soldiers on the instruction of then Home Secretary Winston Churchill had killed the so-called Houndsditch Robbers, who themselves had shot some policemen a couple of weeks earlier. Because the Houndsditch Robbers were terrorists and also of European extraction, the Clapham Common murder became tenuously linked to them. It emerged that the letter 'S' had been carved on both of the murdered man's cheeks.

The case became Sherlock Holmesesque and chimed in with the general mistrust of foreigners that the fermenting situation in Europe had engendered. All non-Brits were now viewed as potential anarchists, which made life in some parts of London, where large immigrant populations had dwelled for generations, pretty uncomfortable. The Bradshaws felt a special local connection with the Morrison case and were relieved when Winston Churchill, again, intervened and commuted his death sentence to life imprisonment. If the baker said Steinie was innocent that was good enough for them.

Macabre murder cases were soon pushed off the front pages as the Germans suddenly arrived in Belgium, and Britain had sent out the army to repel them. It then became apparent that there were not enough men already serving or in reserve to deal with the dreaded German Army, and so Lord Kitchener embarked on his campaign to rally the young male population to the cause. 'Your Country Needs You' he told them as he literally pointed the finger at each and every one in recruitment posters and they enlisted in their thousands at the hastily opened call-up centres up and down the country. Life for Nell, Annie, Battersea and Britain would never be the same after 1914.

Teddy was the first of the family to sign up. The army's initial drive attracted the youngest men and appealed to their natural sense of adventure and camaraderie: whole streets, football teams, old schoolmates and workforces signed up together and Teddy, as an apprentice in the railway yards, was caught up in the euphoria. Never before and never again would so many go to war so enthusiastically. Starting work had been the making of Teddy and it seemed at last he was coming out of himself and enjoying life. He was training to be an engineer and had inherited his grandfather's love of books and reading. His wages were not spent on beer and cigarettes but on books, journals and magazines, and as his knowledge of the world grew so did his confidence. He was a young 18, however, and when he presented himself in his uniform at home, although his mother and sister said they thought he looked a picture, they were both filled with inner sadness. To them, he looked like a young boy dressing up. He was. They took him down to Welbeck's photo studio on Westminster Bridge Road, where he posed in front of a scene depicting the gates of a stately home, for his photograph. Why the studios were so convinced that their working-class customers wanted to be pictured in such an aristocratic environment is a mystery because few would ever have had aspirations to visit a stately home let alone own one. Likewise, the women being photographed were draped in furs they could never own and stood next to ornate fountains and bushes that they would only ever encounter on a day trip to Kew Gardens.

Business at Welbeck's had never been so good, as the soon-to-be soldiers were ferried along to have their photographs taken for posterity by mothers, sisters, wives and girlfriends. Despite the official line that the war would be short-lived, and it was a simple matter of a show of force to push the Germans back, the women of Britain had a private and shared intuition that many of their menfolk would not be coming home for some time. Perhaps ever.

Sam was next up. On the strength of his coming from a line of lightermen, he signed up for the Royal Navy, where he was soon serving on the submarines. William tried to enlist but was told he was too old. He was needed on the river at this important time for trade, as so many young lightermen had gone away to fight.

Tom was back in Peru, apparently working on the construction of a railway crossing the Andes, and would miss the war completely. Henry Knight joined the Royal Engineers as a sapper and informed Nell that within a couple of weeks he would be on a boat heading for France. Like her brother Teddy, she took Henry down to Welbeck's but insisted he wore his best suit and not an army uniform. 'You're no soldier, 'Enry Knight, and you never will be, and why you think you can be I'll be damned.'

'Nell, the country needs us all. Most of us aren't soldiers, but we all have to fight. There is no other way.'

It did not take long for the terror of the war to sink in: thousands of young men began getting killed daily in Europe, and Battersea was largely and very noticeably empty of young males. Besides the misery of bereavement, the changed demographics frightened the womenfolk, who were now beginning to feel very alone and isolated. It wasn't until the men had gone, pondered Nell later, that you realised how much you liked and needed having them around.

'I think we should be married, Nell,' Henry declared while home on leave of duty. 'You know how wars are, I might not come back and I cannot die not having made you my wife.' The horrors of what he had witnessed already had changed him. It normally takes the passing of the years for people to wake up to how precious, fragile and short life is. War accelerates that awakening like nothing else. Henry's proposal didn't come when Nell expected it might, if at all. They were sitting across the table in the main room of the house in Eland Road whilst Annie busied herself in the kitchen area. He looked over to her for a reaction. Nell looked back at him, a look of complete bewilderment on her face.

'Get off with you, you daft bugger.'

As the war progressed and the casualties of the terrible battles began to include people the Bradshaws knew, Nell began to wish she had said yes to Henry. But she still felt she did not love him in the way she was meant to. She did not pine for him like the poets said she should. Her heart did not flutter when he entered the room nor did she feel an overpowering desire for him. She felt no physical desire at all. She believed, therefore, that it was not fair to him to agree to be his wife. Yet, he was a good man. She was comfortable with him and she liked him more than most. Would a man ever enter her life that did those things for her? Would she ever feel for a man in the way her sister did about Tichy Thorogood? Nell wrestled with this for some months but eventually decided that she should marry Henry. If that was what he wanted, then he deserved it. She did not want the image of his poleaxed face when she had rejected him so offhandedly across the dining table burnt into her soul when she laid flowers on his grave.

Towards the end of the war – although nobody knew it was almost the end – Nell and Henry did finally marry. Each time Henry came home on leave, he looked worse: the horror of living amongst fear, death, blood and guts was taking its toll on a gentle man. He was skin and bone and said very little. He'd been gassed, injured by flying shrapnel and had developed a nervous twitch. Many men were no longer coming home at all and Nell felt guilty she had not married him earlier. A wedding was hastily arranged, with a small reception afterwards at the Stanley Arms, where the proprietor kindly allowed them to spend the night in one of the staff rooms upstairs. It was not a big celebration like Sam's had been because Sam, Teddy and Henry's brothers were all away fighting. Tom was still in the Andes somewhere and even Bill was unable to make the reception. But Henry's father was there and so were Annie and Maggs.

When the celebrations had finished and Nell and Henry retired upstairs, they sat on the bed awkwardly, both nervous of what was expected of them in the coming hours. 'Nell, I know you don't feel the way about me like I do about you, and I don't want you to feel you have to do anything you don't want to, and I know you won't. You never do. We'll get into bed and what 'appens 'appens. And if we go to sleep, that'll be fine and dandy. But I want you to know that I love you. Always 'ave and always will. You're a fine woman and I think we are right for each other. And I think that I'm going to come through this war, got a feeling I will, and I'll get my old job back at Arding & Hobbs and I'll get on there. They like me. And we can 'ave a good—'

''Enry,' Nell butted in.

'What?'

'Shut up!'

Although they had lived sixty years between them, two virginities were yielded that night and the intense experience bonded them in a way they could not have imagined. Nell and Henry knew, whatever lay in store, they would never ever take another sexual partner. Twelve hours later, Henry was on a boat back over to France.

The war was never really discussed at home in Battersea and, except for the absence of menfolk, life went on as normal. When Nell read the newspaper to her mother, they steered clear of accounts of battles and who had advanced where and how many losses were suffered. Generally, the people of Battersea did not believe the war would be lost, despite daily evidence of devastated families losing sons, husbands and brothers. They were the Empire. Britain had ruled over a fifth of the world's population. Defeat was inconceivable.

Before the war, it was an event in working-class Battersea households to receive a letter through the post. There were no electricity, gas or telephone bills to anticipate each quarter and there was no junk mail. Therefore, a letter or postcard, when one did arrive, was more often than not a welcome interruption to be passed around the family and shown to neighbours: proof that your family had a life outside of Battersea. The Bradshaws would hear from Tom two or three times a year and occasionally from Aunt Janie and her children and grandchildren. In a community where few travelled more than a few streets away, unless to fight in wars, postcards from other parts of England and the world were a source of great pride; evidence of *getting on*. The war changed all that. People now feared and dreaded a visit from the postman because although he may have been delivering a card from a loved one he was just as likely to be bringing news of a death or a serious injury. It was with such a knot in her stomach that Nell took a letter from the postman one morning near Christmas of 1916. Annie, with her old, wizened face, looked at her daughter mournfully as Nell examined the envelope.

'Postmark is Soufampton,' noted Nell, as fear subsided and curiosity arose.

She took the letter from its envelope and read its brief content:

> We regret to inform you that Edward Bradshaw, formerly of Sleaford Street, Battersea, and Tooting Graveney Union Workhouse, Wandsworth, died on 17 December 1916. He had entered the workhouse here on 23 May 1915. His body has been buried in the grounds of the Southampton Union Workhouse and a small parcel of his belongings is available for collection if you so wish.
>
> Isaac Cribb,
> Governor,
> Southampton Union Workhouse.

She then read it aloud to her mother.

'Soufampton? What's he doing in Soufampton?' asked Annie,

as Nell held the letter, shaking her head and her hand trembling. They had no idea how Edward could have ended up so far away and although this was not what was uppermost in their minds, they discussed it in an effort to mask the shock, guilt and rising sadness they were both feeling.

''E'd of gorn down there to try and get a boat somewhere. I know 'im. 'E must 'ave gathered his strength and gorn down there. 'E was problee trying to go to America,' Annie said eventually.

'I don't think so, Mother. 'E'd 'ave no money. Nowhere to go. 'E problee left Tooting and tramped and that was where 'e ended up. I expect 'e'd gone insane.'

Nell looked up from the letter and noticed her mother's eyes were brimming with tears, feelings from the early years of their marriage and courtship resurfacing; emotions and memories that had been deeply buried. The two women embraced and cried hard, Edward's presence filling the space around them for the first time in years.

Annie did not wish to visit Southampton to collect Edward's belongings, but Nell felt compelled to do so, and took the train up to Waterloo and then changed for the long trip down to Southampton. On the station, she asked a porter the way to the Southampton Union Workhouse, hastening to add she had business there – perish the thought that anyone should think she was *entering* the workhouse. She felt great trepidation about going inside: there was a superstition that those who visited the workhouse would one day become resident. It was a widely held belief when Nell was a child and would surely have contributed to the sense of and actual abandonment suffered by people when they presented themselves at the workhouse gates. They knew the chances of visits were slim. The man at the office, Mr Isaac Cribb, showed Nell her father's grave, although it meant little: it was not marked in any way and it seemed that other bodies had already been added alongside or even on top of Edward's. Mr Cribb handed her a death certificate, showing the cause of death as pneumonia, and a small parcel wrapped in newspaper tied with string. She noticed two other packets similarly presented lying on the table. She thanked him and carried all that remained of her father's life back to the railway station.

On the train home she carefully unwrapped the package and examined its contents. There was his certificate from the Company of Watermen and Lightermen printed on thick parchment to make it more resistant to water. There was a hip flask that would have been confiscated from him on entry and a knife he carried for cutting rope. She recognised the knife from her childhood and held it for a while, as he had done, trying to feel her father for a minute. Finally, there was a gold watch and chain, which she had never seen before. It felt heavy in her hand and was of the type and quality worn by well-to-do people on their waistcoats. Tichy Thorogood had one, but it was not of the calibre of the watch she now threaded through her fingers. She was surprised that Mr Cribb had volunteered it because it clearly had value. The realisation of another human being's basic honesty warmed her and she vowed to write to the man when she was back at home. She then flipped open the cover of the watch's glass face. The dial bore some creases from some old waterlogging and the hands no longer moved. She shook it and held the watch to her ear, but there was no sound of ticking. Before she closed the cover, she noticed an inscription on the inside. She squinted to read it:

Dear Bobby
On Your Coming of Age
Love Father and Mother 1897

It did not take Nell too long to deduce who Bobby was and where the gold watch had come from. Indeed, as she searched back in her mind she could remember reading the newspaper articles aloud to her father and recalled that the young aristocrat whose body was missing on the Thames for those days, all those years ago, was named Robert 'Bobby' Ware. She dropped the watch into her pocket before re-wrapping her father's worldly belongings. She decided she would not, could not, tell her mother about the watch and that her father had robbed the body of a dead man. She didn't want her to think less of her husband than she already did.

X

Their Country Needed Them

Henry sent Nell pretty-coloured postcards from France with embroidered flowers on them, which she kept all of her life. The messages were brief, as Henry was not a great one for writing, and to an outsider they would have seemed most impersonal, but Nell knew differently. She desperately wanted to reply to tell him all about his new baby boy – Henry Patrick Knight – but could not because her husband was moving around. It was tradition to call the eldest boy after his father, but Nell decided she needed also to give back to her grandfather the name he had felt compelled to disown. Henry Patrick it was and what Nell said would go whether her new husband was in France or England. To distinguish the boy from his father, Henry soon became Harry or, more precisely, 'Arry. As Harry grew up his mother told him he had been named after his father, but when he spoke to his uncles they told him he had been named after his uncle, who had perished in the Thames. He drew the conclusion that he had been named after both.

It was 1918 and Annie had stopped going out to work at long last. She now cared for the new baby whilst Nell continued with her job at the pickle factory (having only taken two days off to give birth to Harry), although she did still take in washing and ironing for pin money. There were only three mouths to feed, with Teddy still at war and Maggs never having returned to the family home even though the conflict had seen Maggs and Tichy finally drift apart. Tichy had never gone to fight, claiming first that he was too old and second that he was in 'reserved occupations'. The long-awaited divorce never materialised and his visits to Battersea became less frequent. However, Maggs remained 'Tichy's girl' in the eyes of others and no man seemed inclined to risk walking out with her.

Maggs never said anything directly to Nell or her mother, but it was clear she had become scared of Tichy, and as her girlhood innocence grew into adult wisdom, she had begun to realise that he was a common criminal capable of extreme viciousness and violence. She had met the Italians in Clerkenwell for whom he had worked and began to understand that it was to them that Tichy brought his goods to be sold on and to them he deferred. It was novel for her to see Tichy being told what to do and sucking up to others.

'Who are those men?' Maggs asked innocently once when they jumped on a bus on Farringdon Road, having visited a café on Clerkenwell Green where she had stood around awkwardly as Tichy huddled in a corner with a group of Italian men.

'Ask no questions and you get told no lies,' Tichy quipped, but he volunteered more when Maggs pulled a face and looked away from him. 'They're the Sabinis, gel. They organise a lot of stuff, if yer know what I mean.'

Nell Bradshaw comes of age, 1909.
The aristrocratic backdrop was a far
cry from her real circumstances

Henry Knight, a few years
before the Great War

A Thames lighterman (© National Maritime Museum, London)

Nellie Suttie, who died suddenly
while hop-picking

A postcard from Henry to Nell during the war.

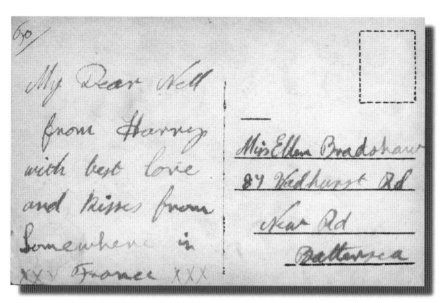

From 'somewhere in France' Henry writes to Nell

Henry returns from war
looking very different,
1919

The letter Nell received from Winston Churchill following her husband Henry's death in July 1919

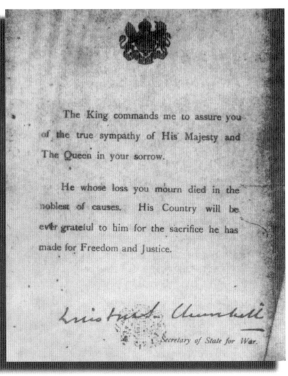

The King commands me to assure you of the true sympathy of His Majesty and The Queen in your sorrow.

He whose loss you mourn died in the noblest of causes. His Country will be ever grateful to him for the sacrifice he has made for Freedom and Justice.

Winston S. Churchill

Secretary of State for War.

Three generations: Nell and her mother Annie with Baby Harry. They are in black because it was taken just after her husband died

Tichy Thorogood and a friend

A day at Hastings, 1925: Maggs, Harry and Nell

At the seaside again, late '20s: Nell
with her son Harry

COAL MINING. DRIVING A HARD HEADING.

A postcard from Tom sent from South Wales while he was mining there

Jim Tregent and Nell Knight on the occasion of their marriage

Winston Churchill surveys bomb damage in Battersea in 1940 (© TopFoto)

Nell Tregent on her 80th birthday

Great-granddaughter Michelle and Nell at the 100th birthday party

Putney Guardian Series, Thursday March 24, 1988

Ellen hits her first century

ELLEN Tregent celebrated her 100th birthday at a party at the Putney Hospital last Saturday.

Mrs Tregent who has a son and numerous grandchildren, has lived in Battersea all her life.

Ellen hits her first century
(© Putney Guardian Series)

'No, I don't know what you mean.'

'What you don't know can't 'urt you, Tichy always says.'

'Oh, don't bother. I don't really care. I was just making conversation.'

'Look, Maggs, I'm not being cute. I can't say too much. They are not nice people, take it from me.'

'Well, if they are not nice people, why are you with them?'

'They're not nice people, but I like 'em.' Tichy's tone of voice had changed, signifying no more was to be said, and he looked hard out of the window.

Another time, when they shared a room in a country hotel following an enjoyable day's racing at Lewes (where Tichy seemed to know everyone), she glimpsed a gun tucked in between his braces and his trousers.

'What is that?' asked Maggs.

'Let's 'ave a look, shall we?' Tichy said, looking down at the protruding butt of the weapon as if it were the first time he had clapped eyes on it. 'Blimey, I'll be blowed – it's a gun. 'Ow did that get there?'

'A gun. Where did it come from? Why do you want a gun?'

Tichy took the gun from his trousers and caressed it in front of her. 'It's called a revolver. A Webley revolver. Ain't it just nice? Our boys bring 'em home from the war and I sell 'em for the lead. I'll get a few guineas for this little beauty.'

'Well, you shouldn't carry a gun around. Does it have bullets? There's enough people dying in the world from guns and bullets, I'm sure.'

'No. I told you. We smelt 'em. Guns are two a penny.'

Tichy continued to caress the gun and looked into the distance beyond her. He lifted the weapon and squeezed an eye shut and aimed it at the mirror. Then he spun around, pretending someone was at the door, and started to jerk as if firing the gun.

'Stop playing with it, then.'

'I told you, it ain't loaded.'

'I should 'ope not, now put it away, it makes me scared.'

Tichy grinned at Maggs's discomfort and fixed her in a stare. 'Did you know, Maggs, that when a man is killed, the murderer's face is left like a photograph on the dead man's eyes. Did you know that? It's true. It's gospel true.'

'That sounds like an old mother's tale to me.'

'Maggs, that's a fact. They keeps it quiet, the perlice do. That's how they catch so many. So, gel, if you decides to kill me one day, you best make sure you shoots my eyes out of their sockets or the perlice will know it's you and you'll be 'ung for sure.'

The thought made Maggs shiver for a second but it was soon lost among the many other far-fetched statements Tichy would make when you were in his company.

He had a thing about black cats too. She remembered him swerving his car to try and run one over once, but, more ominously, there was the time when they were kissing and one scrambled up the fence and sat awhile, watching them. They'd been drinking in the Falcon and were heading home up the hill when Tichy tugged her by the arm into the dark alley that ran up the back of the houses on Lavender Sweep. This was the last opportunity for privacy, before they were illuminated by gaslight and brushed by cars on reaching Eland Road. He pushed her up against a gate and began to kiss her passionately. She could feel the excitement rising up in him and unbuttoned her coat so his hands could wander freely over her. Suddenly, she was aware of the cat staring at Tichy and him staring back at it. He then gently pushed her to one side and stepped forward. ''Ello puss, puss,' he hissed quietly, as if lulling the animal into a false sense of security before unleashing a punch of frightening speed and violence. The cat lurched backwards into the air as if fired from a cannon, emitting a bloodcurdling wail at the same time. Tichy laughed. 'Bet you didn't know cats could fly, did yer, Maggs?'

* * *

Teddy was the first to come home from war. He'd gone away as a boy and came back as a man, both physically and mentally. Although he had had the habit of staring at the walls as a child and spent hour upon hour without speaking, to witness him doing this again as a man was unnerving. He said very little about his experiences and his family did not press him. This was being repeated in families all over Britain. The war had been so horrible, so unimaginably brutal, everyone wanted to bury it as quickly as possible and get back to some sort of normality. Teddy was bitter, though, and when prompted would rail against governments and politicians whom he blamed for the bloodshed.

Sam came home to May and his children and, like his brother Teddy, was also physically unscathed. Truth be told, he enjoyed his war. For the first time, he had been treated as an equal, and he had found he could handle a gun as well as the next man. What he had to offer was the same as everybody else – his life. Unlike a million of his colleagues, he did not have to lay it down. When he returned to Waterloo Station and the concourse was thronged with flag-waving well-wishers, he had never felt so elated or so important. No longer 'Sam, Sam, the Lavatory Man' or 'Poor Sam', he was Sam, the sailor. Sam, the returning hero. Significantly, Teddy never wore his uniform again after he was discharged, but Sam was still wearing his on occasion as late as the mid-'20s.

Brother Bill, who did get called up towards the end of the conflict, so took to navy life that when the war ended he signed up for 12 years and would never take his barge out on the Thames again. His sons, Bill's Bill and Fred, took over from him instead, keeping the line of Bradshaw lightermen afloat. Bill had been invalided out of the navy at one stage when his submarine was torpedoed but had recovered within a year to rejoin and give good service. Although he was away for months on end, his money was secure and the 12 years would qualify him for a sailor's pension. It was a sensible career decision in increasingly uncertain times and was typical of Bill's cautious nature.

Knowing that Henry Knight had also survived the conflict and would be returning to the family to see his new son shortly, Annie and Nell believed that theirs had been an extraordinarily lucky family not to lose anyone in what was already being called the Great War. 'We must be the only family in this street not to 'ave 'ad a letter from the King,' mused Annie one day over dinner.

'Mrs 'Arris, next door to the pub, she lost all three of 'er boys and a brother,' said Nell between chews.

'We haven't lost anyone *yet*,' Teddy corrected with some foresight, 'but everyone has lost something. We've almost killed an entire generation of men and those left behind are suffering as much. I hate to say it, but the effects of this bloody war will last for years and years.'

'We won the war, though. Thank the Good Lord,' Annie replied.

'What have we won, Mum? I can't see the spoils of war, can you? Who were we fighting? Why were we fighting? Do we really know? Who explained to us what we were fighting for? Who told all those boys that they'd probably die or have their arms and legs blown away? I don't think we won anything. It was like we was going 'opping. They got us all excited, put us on trains and let us out on the farms to be shot down by German machine guns. It's not right. People was tricked. Someone should pay. People will pay. It must never happen again. But you know what? It will. As

sure as I sit here with you, it'll happen again and again and again.'
He stood up and walked out of the room, his own rhetoric
making him angry and red in the face. Annie looked over at Nell
and pulled her 'Who rattled his cage?' face.

* * *

The family heard about a basement flat going down at Lurline
Gardens, and Nell and her mother went to look at it. They fell in
love with the place immediately. The houses were 'posh' mansion
blocks broken into flats and backed on to the really well-to-do
houses on Prince of Wales Drive, which in turn looked out over
Battersea Park. Almost next door was a public library. It was
perfect. They were back within spitting distance of Sleaford
Street and only down the road from Sam and May. With Edward
now passed on, they both felt the time was right to move back to
the Dogs Home and river area and make this a new home for
Henry, returning from the war, and young Harry, the son he
hadn't seen, who would now have a father. It also represented an
important shift in the family structure: this was Nell's home and
her mother lived with her rather than the other way round.
However, although there was room for Teddy in the new set-up,
the dynamics of the family had changed, and he felt
uncomfortable with the move and announced that he'd be
moving on shortly.

When Henry returned from France in 1919, there was no
question of him looking for work until his good health had been
restored. Before the war, he had worked at Arding & Hobbs (he
lost his job when the building was destroyed by fire – in his more
mischievous moments, Tichy claimed he had something to do
with this). From there, he took a job as store assistant in Swan &
Edgars and Gamages in London and finally settled at the Army

and Navy store on Oxford Street. They thought well of Henry and shortly before he enlisted he had won promotion to floor manager. Nell had been up to the Army and Navy on Henry's behalf and returned with the news that they were ready to take him back just as soon as he was fit. Arding & Hobbs had been rebuilt and was flourishing again.

One day, while looking through the old biscuit tin in which Henry kept his things, Nell came across a letter that her husband had written whilst away at war, which he had hoped would have been passed to her should he have perished in action. He kept it in the tin along with a few other odd belongings and mementoes. As she sat down and read it, she cried, wiping away her tears with her apron. Then she folded it back up and replaced it without mentioning a thing to Henry. It read simply:

> Dearest Nell,
>
> If this letter finds you I reckon I am not coming home. Please do not morn me for a long time and tell young Henry about the good times and to think of me with a smile allways. Tell him how you made me so happy becarse you did make me happy Nell. Like you do most people. You are a grand lady and I treasure the time we had it pains me to part but I have every faith we will join together again in the next life. Until then please live the one you are living to the full. Your picture is still next to my hart. Fondest love to Mother and kiss little Henry for me every singel day.
>
> Yours for ever and ever,
> Henry

As the summer came to an end, Henry spent more time in his bed at Lurline Gardens than out of it. Nell and Annie's attempts to build him up were not working. Copious amounts of cod liver oil, brandy, stout and 'restorative' pills ordered from dubious advertisements in newspapers were having no beneficial effect. He was 'under the doctor', however, and they had confidence in his belief that Henry was merely weak from the war and time would heal him. One small blessing of his declining health, Nell always thought, was that it enabled him to bond with his baby son, Harry, and spend time lots of time with him. He tended to and played with his child in a way Nell would not see a father do again for a couple of generations. He changed, cleaned and fed baby Harry in such a caring and tender manner that Nell would have to fight back tears at the thought of it 60 years later. Eventually, Nell realised, as did Henry, that he was getting weaker all the time and that the doctors were wrong. He was dying. For each other's sakes, they continued the charade that he was on the mend.

When winter arrived, Henry succumbed to the influenza virus that had been ravaging the elderly, the young and the infirm of London since the previous year. He took on a fever and the doctor ordered immediately that he be admitted to the Millbank soldiers' hospital over the river. The doctor said it was primarily to protect others in the house from catching the flu from Henry, but Nell knew as she helped her gaunt, sweating and trembling husband into the back of the doctor's car that he would not be coming home.

'You be a good boy, Harry,' he whispered as he kissed his son, Annie lifting the baby up so Henry did not have to bend down.

'Daddy,' gurgled the toddler.

'Look after your mum and your nanny when you're a big boy, won't you?' Henry said, as he gently stroked his son's forehead.

Nell and Annie felt tears well up in their eyes at this final remark, for it was proof that Henry knew he was not coming home. He was to last only three more days on a ward with other dying ex-soldiers.

Henry had a corner bed and Nell looked out onto the river as her husband ebbed in and out of consciousness. Lightermen were still out there in their numbers, despite the growth in motorised vehicles and rail transport, negotiating the sets with their sweeps just as her brother, father and grandfather had done. Not far upstream was the bridge where her youngest sibling had been swallowed by the greedy river and downstream was the bank where Edward had discovered the drowned body of Bobby Ware, an event that had changed so many lives for ever. Never before had she felt so acutely the power the Thames held over her family and she wondered what, if anything, it could have in store for them now. Her eyes rested on Henry as he struggled for breath and his pigeon-chest rose and quivered in anticipation of an intake of air. She grieved for the life they would not now have. Theirs was a love story back to front. No love at first sight, weak knees or pounding hearts; instead, a slow-burning friendship that grew into courting and then finally tumbled over into love. The momentum had been rudely interrupted by the war and would now be finally terminated by Henry's death. Nell knew that their love would have grown stronger, that Henry would have risen in his job and their family would have been a close, stable and happy one. They would have *got on* in life. She felt sorry for herself, but she felt nothing but the deepest aching sorrow for Henry, who was having everything taken away from him.

'All right, my sweetheart?' smiled Henry, as he fought through the haze to consciousness.

Such a lovely, all-conquering smile, thought Nell. 'I'm fine, darling.' She squeezed his hand and was shocked by the strength he exerted in squeezing hers. ''Enry, can you 'ear me? I've got somefing to tell you. I'm expecting. Expecting a baby. I'm going to call it Edward, after my father.'

Henry's smiled broadened and he managed to lift his head slightly off the pillow as he tugged on Nell's hand. 'Let's 'ope for a boy, then.'

XI

The Lady and the lady

It is Christmas Day in the workhouse,
And the cold, bare walls are bright
With garlands of green and holly,
And the place is a pleasant sight;
For with clean-washed hands and faces,
In a long and hungry line
The paupers sit at the table,
For this is the hour they dine.

The first time Nell heard this was down at the Grand before her father died and she enjoyed it as much as the rest of the audience. It was very popular with the music-hall crowds. Over the years, it became part of the staple diet of home entertainment at Christmas as one family member or another stood up to recite it in full once the post-dinner drink had begun to flow. It gained popularity as the threat of the workhouse receded and the stark reality of its existence became a memory, with fewer and fewer people having had the misfortune of direct experience. Eventually, music-hall entertainers such as Billy Bennett and Stanley Holloway were able to juggle with the words and produce humorous skits – the message having lost its original social and emotional impact.

After her father died, Nell would not allow the poem to be spoken in her house and if she was in a room where it was being recited, she would leave, so painful were the memories and so poignant the words to her. These were hard times for Nell and visits to the music hall had become scarce. She was under pressure both mentally and economically. She had lost a father and a husband and gained two dependants in the space of five years. Her mother was no longer bringing money into the house and although her brother Teddy had decided to stay at home and support his sister during this time, he was himself finding work harder and harder to come by. Her second child, born in early 1920, was indeed a boy, as she knew it would be, and she gave him her father's name, as she said she would. Edward soon became Ted, though, and her boys became the focus of her life. She vowed to make sure that, even though they were ''alf an orphan', her sons would receive a good education and get on in life.

Letters from King George and Winston Churchill, then Secretary of State for War, expressing their condolences at Henry's death meant very little to Nell at the time and were folded up and sealed in the biscuit tin, but in later life she drew some comfort from them and they began to see the light of day. She liked to think that the politician and monarch felt a genuine sadness at her husband's death and that Henry really had achieved something by drawing those famous and powerful men's sympathies.

The Lady and the lady

Annie continued to stay at home looking after the baby boys whilst Nell was forced to leave her job at the pickle factory and built up a portfolio of cleaning jobs that paid more money in total than she had received from Messrs Crosse & Blackwell. Each morning, she would rise at 5 a.m. and take the tram down the Embankment to the offices of an insurance company in Westminster. From there, she would visit various large houses, where she carried out domestic cleaning and charring. She soon built up a regular list of upper-class clients in the Chelsea, Westminster and Knightsbridge areas who could not quite justify full-time servants but felt unable to clean their own homes. In the evening, she was back up in the City, scrubbing more offices. Nell was never home before 9 p.m. and often went straight to her bed exhausted.

During this time, with the loss of her husband and her father still raw, Nell often reflected on how life had unfolded for the family. She got to musing on the reward money and how that had become a turning point for her father, her mother and all of the children. She had heard her mother say to her father before that the reward money was the devil's money but was never quite sure why. Perhaps Annie knew that Edward had taken the gold watch from the dead boy after all and had therefore tainted the reward. She couldn't be sure. She started to feel that the gold watch, now hidden in her own Huntley and Palmers biscuit tin on top of the wardrobe with her other valuables, was a symbol of the things that had gone wrong for the Bradshaws. Her never-far-below-the-surface superstitious emotions came to the fore and she became convinced that she would not rest until she had handed back the watch to the dead boy's parents. Only then, she believed, would her family's lives and luck improve. Never before had she been so sure she had to do something.

There was only one Lord Ware in the pre-war *Who's Who* directory she consulted in the library in Lurline Gardens and she decided that he must be the drowned boy's father. The Wares were based in a place called Docking Hall and on consulting a map she located the village of Docking in the northernmost point of rural Norfolk. Early one Saturday morning, without telling Annie or Teddy the truth – she said she was enquiring about a job – she set off from Liverpool Street to King's Lynn on the train and then took a small branch line to Docking. It was the first time she had headed north out of London in her life. She noted how different the landscape looked to the only other countryside she had ever experienced: that of Sussex and Kent. Miles of green and yellow rolling farmland extended to the horizon from the train window and not an oast-house or copse in sight.

When she alighted from the train – the sole passenger to do so at this tiny and deserted station – and walked out into the village, she headed straight for the pub across the road from the station. A few locals, who she took to be farm labourers, nursed jugs of beer and studied her as she walked to the bar.

'Could you tell me where Docking Hall is?' she asked of the publican.

'Yes, ma'am. Just foller the road up, and past the old church turn left and there it is front of you. You'll see the entrance just a little bit down the way. You can't miss it, my dear.'

'Thank you.'

'And may I ask what business you might have at Docking Hall?' enquired the publican, assuming that a new housekeeper or servant was going to be taking up residence in the village but not understanding why a lady from as far away as London would be taking up the post.

'No, you may not, but you can pour me a glass of Guinness.'

The Lady and the lady

The farm labourers exchanged wry glances.

Docking Hall was small as country piles go but was nevertheless imposing, standing at the front of a sweep of farmland extending as far as the eye could see. A maid, who looked Nell up and down in the way she only would a person she recognised immediately as her social equal, answered the door.

'I'd like to see Lord Ware.'

The maid's face dropped a little and she searched for the right words, 'He's not here. Madam is, though. Would you like to see her? Who shall I say is calling?'

'Tell 'er it's Mrs Knight from Battersea and I 'ave some information concerning 'er Bobby.'

The maid's face changed from embarrassment to shock and she almost ran indoors to fetch her mistress. Lady Ware was dressed elegantly in the sort of fine clothes and sparkling brooches Nell and her like only wore when they visited the photographer's studio. She was tall with a long but kindly face and thin lips that were so white they were barely distinguishable from the skin on her face. She smiled sweetly at Nell as she led her to a lounge where she sat down awkwardly on the edge of a sofa that looked like it was covered in silk.

'Would you like a drink, Mrs Knight?'

'I could murder a cup of tea.'

The maid scampered off to fetch the refreshment.

'My husband died six years ago,' Lady Ware explained.

'Snap, so did mine.'

Lady Ware was taken aback by the turn of phrase used by this woman. Her curiosity was pumping her heart. They exchanged some small talk about their respective losses until the maid arrived back with a silver tray, a teapot and two cups and saucers. Sugar was in lumps in a bowl. When the maid had left the room and she had sipped her tea, Nell fished into her overcoat, pulled out the watch and gently spread it on the coffee table between them. Lady Ware recognised the piece immediately and dramatically held it to her breast before reading the inscription for the first time in a quarter of a century.

'Who are you, Mrs Knight?' she gasped.

Nell explained the story, as she knew it, barely stopping for breath and refilling her tea cup herself as Lady Ware sat transfixed, not saying a word, totally bewitched by the cockney lady sitting opposite her and the unfolding story. Nell told of Edward's drinking once he was in receipt of the reward money; how her mother never approved of the money and they had rowed badly when he was in drink; how poor Henry had perished in the river and Sam blamed himself; how they all ran away from their father and he ended his days lonely and unloved in the poorhouse; and then how her own Henry had died from pneumonia in the Millbank hospital after fighting in the war; and that she knew she had to get this watch back to the parents of Bobby Ware before her family's luck could possibly change.

When she was done, Lady Ware came across to Nell and sat down beside her, taking her hand into hers and squeezing it. 'Mrs Knight . . . may I call you Nell? Nell, I have so much to say to you. Firstly, you don't know how much this means to me. You really don't. You have made me so happy today and I don't know how I could ever repay you. What you don't know, I imagine, is that it is almost twenty years ago to the day that we lost poor Bobby. Over the last few days, he has been on my mind more than usual and I have been praying to the Lord for a sign that he is at peace and that he and his father are reunited in heaven and are waiting for me. I have been down at the church there, on my knees beseeching God, to give me that comfort. Lo and behold, you arrive at the house with this. I could not have dreamt of a more telling intervention. You have brought me a peace today that I doubted I would ever find and I thank you from the bottom of my heart.

'Secondly, you must understand that your father did nothing wrong in my estimation. He yielded to temptation, as we all do sometimes in our life, but I think it speaks a lot that he never ever sold the watch. He took it but almost certainly regretted it from the first day. Why your mother believed the reward to be tainted in some way I do not understand, especially if you say she does not know about this watch. Maybe she does and has not told you. Whatever, you must not believe that the watch, the demise of your parents' union and his drinking are all connected. They certainly are not. I do not know the details of your mother's life, but from what you tell me she had a hard time, as you have had, Nell, and when people suffer unhappiness and disillusionment, it is easy to blame an event or a person or even an object such as this. I think that is what has happened here and you are now repeating your mother's superstition. I would like to meet your mother and put her mind to rest.'

'You wouldn't. You couldn't. She 'asn't got the sort of mind that can be put at rest.'

They both laughed at this.

'Nell, you've come halfway across the country today. I won't hear of you going home this afternoon. Please spend the rest of the day with me and stay the night. We can drive you in the morning to King's Lynn for a train.'

'Oh, Gawd no, nobody knows I'm 'ere. I need to get back for tonight or they'll worry.'

'Can't we telephone them?'

'We don't 'ave a telephone.'

'Do any of the neighbours have a telephone?'

'No.'

145

The two ladies talked for an hour or two longer, Lady Ware telling Nell all about her son's short but eventful life and Nell describing young Henry's even shorter time on earth. Although the two boys inhabited different worlds, the two women were moved to tears again as they silently contemplated the irony and circumstances of their deaths. They laughed and cried and found great comfort in one another, and exchanged postal addresses so they could correspond in the future. Lady Ware arranged for her driver to take Nell to King's Lynn to catch the train back to London. From her bureau, where she had written out her address for Nell, she fiddled and then handed Nell another envelope. 'This is a small token of my appreciation,' she said as she held the envelope out to Nell.

'You're 'aving a joke, I 'ope! This is 'ow all this started, whatever you say. It ends 'ere. I don't want nuffin' from you. Thanks all the same, my lady.'

Lady Ware smiled again and pulled Nell towards her, and the two women embraced. 'If you're ever up this way, be sure to call in,' Lady Ware called as she waved Nell off.

'When am I going to be up this way again?' thought Nell, but she waved and smiled back. She then settled into the back seat of the gleaming Rolls-Royce and fingered the leather as the car weaved through the country lanes towards King's Lynn.

'When you're hungry or need to stop for the toilet, just let me know,' said the chauffeur.

'Why? Is the station a long way?'

'No, Lady Ware has told me to drive you back to London. We could be on the road for five to six hours.'

And that is how late one dusky evening in 1925 Nell Bradshaw arrived on the Battersea Park Road in a chauffeur-driven Rolls-Royce and stepped out into the yellow gaslight. To her eternal disappointment, the only person she knew that caught the historic moment was Annie Mitchell from number 11, and she was returning from the pub and never asked how or why. Nell can only assume she was pie-eyed and thought she had imagined it.

XII

Charlie and the Fruit Shop

Whilst Nell was drawing some bad cards, her sister's life had begun to take a turn for the better. Tichy had now fully disappeared from view. She did not see him for over a year during the war and infrequently at other times. In 1918, she had been told by a mutual friend that he was 'breaking rocks on the moor', although she never found out for what offence he was finally incarcerated. The last time she ever saw him to talk to was on Lavender Hill and he seemed uncharacteristically embarrassed to have bumped into her. It was around 1921 and she noted for the first time that he had aged. Some of the muscle around his midriff had turned to fat and flecks of grey had peppered his hair. He said he was now in the 'motor-car game' and had taken some premises up on St John's Hill. He offered no explanation for his lack of contact.

'Well, it's good to see you, Maggs, and you're looking fine. Still a real picture, you are. I 'eard about Nell's 'Enry. Sorry to 'ear that.

'E was a good boy. But Nell'll be all right. Strong as an ox, that one. Although it will be a brave man that takes 'er on and two nippers. I must be shooting away, Maggs, got to see a man about a car. You know 'ow it is for Tichy. Always on the go.'

Maggs was almost delighting in his discomfort. She could tell that the spark he had for her had gone and was relieved when she realised that the one she held for him was almost extinguished too. When he got into a car parked on the corner of Lavender Sweep, she could see why he was so on edge: sitting in the passenger seat, waiting patiently, twisting ringlets of hair around her finger, was a girl. She couldn't have been a day over 18.

By this time, Maggs had become friendly with a youngish man who worked in the greengrocer's shop near her home on the Wandsworth Road. She had noticed him noticing her. He wore a permanent grin and had the air of a man constantly a breath or two away from laughter. One day, she walked around him as he laid the vegetables out on the trestle tables in front of the shop. She just knew that he had stopped what he was doing and was staring at her walking away. When she turned, her instinct was confirmed and they exchanged shy and knowing smiles before looking away. The next day, Maggs came into the shop, as she occasionally did, and the young man spoke.

'I'm Charlie. My father owns this shop and he has a second on St John's Hill, where he works out of. He gives me a free hand running this one. If you're ever looking for work, I'm looking for someone to help me.'

He had gathered that Maggs was single but could not understand why and had felt a strong attraction the first time she had entered the shop. When Maggs left the shop, she glanced backwards at the sign above the big display window – C. E. Melchior, Greengrocers and Fruiterers – and for the first time the pleasant young man registered with her.

Charlie and the Fruit Shop

She started working Saturdays with Charlie. They made a great team and soon drifted into becoming a couple. Maggs was good for business. She had a head for figures and was cute with the customers. Her good looks were pulling men in to buy items of fruit they would never normally have dreamt of purchasing. She could be outrageously flirtatious, which bothered Charlie a little until he realised it meant nothing to Maggs and it was just jealousy he was feeling. Anyway, she could carry it off so well.

'I bet you'd like a nice pear, sir.' If Charlie heard it from Maggs once, he heard it a hundred times. Men would happily pay a tanner just to hear her utter the phrase.

He came around to meet her family and she his and everyone thoroughly approved. After Tichy, the Bradshaws could not have been more delighted: here was a respectable, law-abiding, gentle and funny man who was the heir to a couple of shops. What more could they want for Maggs? Charlie was a livewire too – Annie said he could talk the hind legs off a donkey – and was forever on the move. Sometimes, he'd run the couple of miles between the two shops and back just to get a bag of loose change. He owned a small van in which he and his father would go up to Covent Garden market to buy their fruit and vegetables and out into the Surrey countryside to pick up fresh farm produce daily. Maggs was soon aware that Charlie had fallen for her and although she did not have the same feeling for him in the same passionate engulfing and often painful way she had for Tichy, she was becoming fonder and fonder of the young shopkeeper.

Maggs and Charlie tied the knot in 1922 at the St George's church up near Nine Elms. It was a good Bradshaw wedding, with drink flowing and loud singing into the night at the Mason's Arms, where the reception was held. A decade or so on from Sam's wedding, Nell reflected on the changes in the family. Bill was still at sea, sending money home for Dolly and the children, who were grown up or growing up fast, and was unable to make the wedding. Tom, too, was away. As always. The last letter they'd received was from Poona in India, but Tom was vague with the detail. What he was doing and who with remained a mystery. Nell still missed Tom and wished he would come home and settle down. After all, he was nearly 40, not some young kid. Teddy, too, was away. Not a great turnout from the Bradshaws for Maggs's big day, but there were plenty of relatives on the Melchior side and most of them shared Charlie's upbeat, happy nature and the two Battersea families connected well. A cousin of Charlie's, a cheesemonger from Kentish Town, paid Nell a great deal of attention all evening and even asked if he could see her again. She refused but was nevertheless flattered and cheered by the attention. It warmed Nell's heart most, though, to see her sister so happy and Nell was glad that the spectre of that rogue Tichy Thorogood had disappeared at long last from her life.

Teddy had left home a few months before. He had become bitter and increasingly unhappy. As the war receded in the collective memory a little, it took on a larger and larger proportion in his. He believed that the common people had been used as cannon fodder by the ruling classes, and the loss of life and suffering were totally unnecessary. He was not sure quite who to blame: politicians were the main subject of his wrath but at times it was also the Royal Family. These latter sentiments did not go down well with Annie or Nell, and Teddy became more frustrated at what he felt (but never said) was their ignorance on such important matters. He had not worked for some months before he left, although Annie and Nell were not sure how hard he was trying. Instead, he consumed more and more books and pamphlets about labour struggles, politics, economics and history, and attended many speeches being made by local and national activists of the left-wing persuasion.

Teddy hoped that the working classes and poor were slowly but surely gaining some momentum in upsetting the status quo of the country and that the fundamental injustices of the class system were imminently going to crumble. He became animated about various strikes that were now regularly cropping up around the land and refused to see them in isolation. Like many, he viewed the formation of the Labour Party as a huge step forwards and believed it was only a matter of time before those politicians formed a government. Revolution was in the sooty air he was breathing, although his feelings were not universally shared.

'But, Teddy, if there were no rich people, 'oose 'ouses would we clean? If there were no big corporations, 'oo'd pay the workers, 'oo'd produce the goods? 'Oo'd run the country? You need to be educated to do that.' The first few times, he tried to explain to his mother and sister that it was those very assumptions and beliefs that he and others were trying to overcome. Their servility and the happy acceptance of their lot in life appalled him.

'We don't help ourselves, Mum. We've got to stop all this forelock tugging. Why don't we have a good education? Have you ever wondered that? Why should some people live in big houses and others live like this?'

'Like this!' Annie exclaimed, her voice quivering with offence. 'What d'you mean, like this? We live very well, thank you, son. We've 'ad good lives. When 'ave you ever had to go without a meal? When 'ave you starved?'

'We have not had good lives, Mum,' Teddy replied quietly and calmly, already knowing he would not be able to convince his mother and sister. 'That's what they want us to think. We nearly got wiped out in the war. We labour for the upper classes and we're meant to be grateful of the few pennies they throw us. Mum, we're no better than the slaves in America.'

''Ow dare you! If you weren't my son, I'd throw you out of this 'ouse. Saying we are no better than nigger slaves.'

'I meant we are treated no better than slaves, Mum.' Teddy ended the argument with some desperation in his voice and shook his head. Realising there was no mileage in attempting to convert his family to the cause, he eventually gave up and found his outlet with like-minded people who convened in halls and pubs around Battersea and beyond.

He joined the Labour Party and attended every march or demonstration in London. Some must have turned nasty because more than once he returned home with cuts and bruises. Teddy would always insist that the police had been brutal.

'Teddy,' said his mother once, 'I don't understand 'ow you expect to find work when you're always going to meetings and marches about not 'aving any work.'

'That's what they want, isn't it? They want people like me to sit at home fretting or being too busy in some low-paid slavery job so we can't form a group and fight together for the common good.'

'Son, if there is one thing I've learnt in this world that is you 'ave to look after yerself because nobody else will.'

'Well, they will and they can. That's where you are wrong. Only in groups can we have power. Divide and rule, that's what they want, and we ain't going to let them get away with it any longer.'

'Oh, shut up, son. Let's have a cup of tea.'

He didn't leave home as such. One day he told his mother and sister that he was going to travel the country getting work where he could.

'But there's work 'ere, Teddy,' Annie told him. 'There's work on the railways, on the river and in the factories.' She could remember saying much the same thing to Tom when he set off on his adventures.

'I know, Mum. I want to see the country, that's all. I need to find out what people are feeling. I need to see what is happening. I can't explain it, but it's something I have to do. Don't worry, I'll not be like our Tom. I'll be back.'

Nell felt less upset about Teddy going than Tom all those years before. She thought a bit of travel would do him good and help him shake off his demons. The irony would be that Tom did come home – Teddy never would.

Annie walked over to Clapham Junction with her son the day he left. He was vague about his first destination but said he was heading north. He had some money saved. When Annie kissed him on the forehead as she left him outside the station entrance, she could not have guessed in a hundred years that it would be the last time she'd set eyes on her troubled little boy.

Despite a worsening national economic situation, the shops belonging to Charlie Melchior's father prospered. The premises on St John's Hill was the more successful, since it benefited from the increasing patronisation of the Clapham Junction railway complex and picked up a great deal of transient trade. The shop on the Wandsworth Road relied heavily on local custom, but Charlie senior was pleased that takings and profits had improved steadily since his son and his young wife had been operating it. Young Charlie had always been slow to get his customers to settle their credit or 'tick', but Maggs had the knack of collecting without alienating the customers. She had also encouraged Charlie to launch a delivery round in the fast-growing and more affluent commuter areas of Wimbledon, Raynes Park and Kingston. It was an immediate hit, bringing in new revenue and new customers. In 1925, Charlie senior made his son a partner in the business, with all the profits from the Wandsworth Road shop going to Charlie and those from the round being split in half. Charlie senior kept the profits from Clapham Junction. Young Charlie was now a man of means with energy and drive to burn.

Maggs now found herself a partner in a thriving small business and, truth be told, she was the dominant partner in both the marriage and the business. She often complained that her husband was too soft and too nice and did not have a head for business. Charlie was happy for his wife to take the lead and would rarely argue with her or go against anything she said. Nell said privately that the way he would sometimes sit and look at her, lost in admiration and adoration, reminded her of her sister 15 years earlier in the company of Tichy Thorogood. She remembered feeling sorry for him one day when the delivery boy let slip that Charlie had a custom of throwing small packets of groceries and cigarettes over the wall of Wandsworth Prison for the inmates to pick up. Maggs tore into him. 'Why in God's name are you throwing our profits over the prison wall, Charlie Melchior?'

'It's only bits and pieces, Maggs. Poor sods need something other than gruel.'

'They're in prison because they've done wrong. And you know what, if they catch you throwing them food and fags, they'll put you in there with 'em. And you know what, there'll be no bleedin' idiot throwing anything over the wall for you.'

Maggs's new-found prosperity was quickly spread around the family and all of her siblings' households received baskets of fruit and vegetables on a weekly basis as part of Charlie's round. Also the small Melchior van was used to pack in the children and take them to the seaside resorts of southern England. Previously, Annie had only ever been to Kent for the hopping, to Hastings a handful of times on day trips and to Epsom for the Derby. Now, she was visiting Margate, Brighton, Folkestone, Deal and Dover. On the way home, they were stopping in beautiful English gardens and having cream tea.

''Ow nice of these people to let us in their gardens and then bring us out tea,' she marvelled. For her, a whole new world had belatedly but pleasantly opened up.

Ted and Harry, Nell's boys, who had no father to look up to, became close to Charlie and he to them. Both boys spent as much time at the shop, in the van and at the Melchiors' house as they did at home, which was a help to Nell: she was still hard at work each day and Annie was becoming increasingly frail in her old age. The reality was that the two young Knight boys were fending for themselves from a very young age and although Nell was under the impression they were being watched by her mother, they were out and about on the trams, trains and buses, and on the streets most of the day. By now, Annie spent more time having 'her nap' than she did awake.

In June 1927, Annie was strong enough to attend the Epsom Derby. To the boys' delight, Uncle Tom was home – he had entered the house unannounced the night before and thrown all his loose change in the air for them to scamper after. Nell could remember her father doing the very same thing. He insisted they all travel down to Epsom together the following day for the Derby.

It was a large party that gathered on the platform at Clapham Junction: Sam and May and their children; Bill's Dolly and their young children; Maggs and Charlie; and Tom, Annie, Nell and the boys. The train was packed solid and people discussed the horses and where their money was going all the way down to Epsom. Derby Day was always the first Wednesday in June and was an unofficial bank holiday for Londoners. By hook or by crook, they got themselves onto Epsom Downs to absorb the day's racing and the atmosphere. They came on trains, trams and buses, in cars and on foot. All the routes into the Surrey town were blocked from mid-morning. Once a 'posi', a patch of grass on the slope facing the racecourse, was found, blankets and coats were laid down and home base was declared. The men would then wander off to the white beer tents whilst the women would open up the picnic and try to keep the children, who would be hankering to get into the large funfair that groaned and whirled beside them, drawing them like a magnet, on a rein.

Nell put a small bet on Steve Donoghue's ride.

'Steve loves 'orses,' she would always say, as if that explained anything. It was a statement her sons found illogical, as he seemed to whip the animals quite ferociously as the race hotted up. Tom told them not to take any notice of their mother, she wouldn't know one end of a horse from another, and put a tosheroon each on a horse named Call Boy for them. When it won, they were ecstatic and a good deal richer. It was their first Derby, but they were hooked. Why do people starve and why do people go out on strike over money when it is as easy to come by as this? thought young Ted. They adjourned to the heaving Downs Hotel flush with cash and formed a human chain as Tom passed the Guinnesses and bottles of pop from the bar to his family outside.

Only a couple of months after that memorable day out in Epsom, Annie had popped out of the house to collect some shopping whilst the boys were at school. It had been raining and as she crossed Battersea Park Road on her way home from a visit to the haberdashery, she slipped on a wet tramline and broke a hip and a leg. She was taken to St John's Hospital, where she lost consciousness and died the following day. She was just approaching her 70th year. In her shopping bag was her purse which contained a few pennies, a packet of buttons and some thread. Nothing else. It was a shopping trip that the old lady had not needed to take.

XIII

It's Murder

Nell had never felt more alone, having shared a couple of small rooms with her mother for forty-odd years, and the enormity of raising two sons as a widow alone bore down heavily on her. Because of her mother's constant close proximity, it took her death to make Nell appreciate how much she relied on Annie and how much she loved her. Annie could be hard sometimes and could cut up rough with her tongue, but her character had been shaped by her environment. It was simple: you needed to be tough to survive. Not many women got up and left their husbands in her day, especially if there was no other man to go to. Nor did many women manage to raise a family almost single-handedly. Annie was not a tactile person, was not one to make outward demonstrations of affection, but her devotion to her family was total and with Nell's boys she had finally relaxed and enjoyed them.

Harry and Ted remember her as a wonderful grandmother with

a mischievous streak. They certainly saw the best of her. When Charlie Melchior came to the house and was in full swing with a story or two, she would sometimes allow her chin to fall onto her chest and pretend she was asleep. She could be particularly rude to any officials that had cause to visit the house and when visiting her father's grave in Clapham she routinely moved flowers from neighbouring graves to adorn his unmarked spot. The brothers' favourite memory, often retold, was the time they were all awoken at 4.30 one winter's morning to an urgent rapping at their front door. Although she was the eldest member of the household, it was Annie that rose to answer it. But there was nobody there, so Annie returned to her bed.

'Bloody kids,' she grunted. The boys wondered which kids could possibly be playing Knock Down Ginger at this unearthly hour. The incident was forgotten until exactly the same thing happened at exactly the same time the following morning. This time Annie got to the door to see a man running away.

'Can you believe it? A bleedin' man. What does he think 'e's playing at? I'll wring 'is bleedin' neck if he tries that trick again.'

'Do you think we should tell the perlice?' Nell suggested.

'No, I'm going to get up early and wait by the front door for the bugger termorrer morning.'

'You think 'e'll be back?'

'Well, we'll find out, won't we?'

The next morning, Annie was awake and dressed at 4 a.m. and by 4.30 so was everyone else, she made that much racket. Fortified by cocoa, she sat and waited like a cat ready to pounce. She had heard the steps approach the front door. With one hand, she burst it open and with the other, struck the man on the forearm with the poker she was brandishing.

'What the 'ell are you playing at?' screamed the man as he fell to his knees, clutching his stunned and now limp limb.

'What the bleedin' 'ell are *you* playing at, you bleedin' rascal? Knocking at my door every morning and running away. You should know better at your age.'

The man rushed to get his words out before the insane old lady struck him again. 'I'm giving Albert a knock. 'E asked me to,' the man pleaded, utterly confused by the turn of events. 'I work at the dairy with 'im. I'm a milkman too.'

'What you on about? You stark raving mad? 'Oo's Albert?' Annie gave him another tap with the poker for good measure.

As Nell had by now guessed it was a case of mistaken identity and address, and the man was behaving quite innocently in giving his milkman colleague a wake-up call, since he started at the dairy half an hour later. He had the right number but the wrong road.

Instead of apologising for the misunderstanding, though, Annie continued to wave the poker around and sent him on his way with 'And if you ever come back 'ere banging on our door, next time I'll poke this right up your Khyber!'

Things were certainly quieter without Annie. Nell even reluctantly considered the notion of remarrying. It was the last thing she wanted to do, but if it meant a better life for her boys then it was a possible means to an end. She ran through some likely candidates in her mind. There was Jim Tregent from Corunna Street. He was well into middle age now and lived alone with his father. There was not a flicker of romantic attraction on either side, but he did have a well-paid printing job with the *Evening News*. He was plump with big bushy eyebrows and to her resembled the comedian George Robey, albeit without the music-hall man's propensity for mirth. She'd never seen Jim Tregent dare break into a smile. But in conversations they'd occasionally had in the street she had detected the seeds of interest. His father was elderly and Jim would like someone to look after him.

'It must be 'ard for you, Nell, with 'Enry gone and your two nippers,' he fished once.

'It's 'ard for everyone these days, Jim,' was how she had deflected him. But the enquiry was not lost on her. He worked nights. That was a plus. There'd be little opportunity for any funny business.

Willie, one of her late husband's brothers, was now eligible, with his poor wife having died in childbirth. He'd had an insurance policy on her life. She soon dismissed that, knowing it would not have pleased Henry. Of course, there was Frankie Mitchell, Annie Mitchell's eldest, almost ten years younger than Nell, but he had clearly shown an interest in her. One night in the Mason's Arms he had sidled up beside her and whispered, 'Nell Knight, you're built like a thoroughbred racehorse, you are. It's a crime you ain't got an 'usband. A fine woman like you needs a man.'

Nell had taken this as a compliment, even a veiled proposal, despite telling him to clear off before she boxed his ears. Many would not have. However, Frankie drank his money like his dad before him and it would surely take him off early like his father. She liked him, though; but the thought of lying down with him amid the fumes of brown and mild repulsed her.

There was little in the way of practical help from her brothers and sister. As the 1920s progressed, work was becoming harder and harder to find and each of them was fighting their own personal battle for survival. Even Charlie and Maggs's shop was now feeling the pinch, as customers shunned fruit and preferred to scour the market for their vegetables, with money becoming tighter and tighter. It didn't help that within the space of five years they had also produced four children: Charlie (Charlie Boy forever after), young Nell, Violet and Mary. It was a burden rather than a financial boon for Charlie and Maggs when

Charlie Melchior senior succumbed to emphysema in 1931 and the young couple took over the entire business and both shops.

Bill was probably the most secure of the Bradshaws. Having finished his stint in the Royal Navy, he was now in receipt of a regular pension. That was a godsend because work for a man over 50 was impossible to find. He was not inclined to go back out on the river, even if he believed that the trade still existed to warrant it. His son, Bill, was making a living as a lighterman, but he encouraged his younger children to find alternative work and managed to persuade two of his boys to join the navy, as he had. 'Get a pension and learn a trade,' he told them. 'Twelve years is nothing, believe me, it's over before you know it.' He still had his worries, though. There were still three children to support and there were rumblings, as the economy worsened, that the pensions of ex-servicemen would be cut.

Tom, too, was facing difficulty in securing an income, despite his mobility and his lack of dependants, now he was back in England permanently. His sojourns to find work were now nearer to home and shorter-lived. 'The older I get the 'arder I 'ave to bloody work,' he complained.

In Battersea and all over London, money had been found to clear the areas being called slums – but which Battersea people had been happy to call homes for generations – and to erect blocks of council flats in their stead. Tom managed to latch on to the firms building these houses and flats and get work as a hod-carrier but found having to continually graft that much harder to stave off the competition from younger and fitter men took its toll on his constitution.

Every now and then, details of Tom's chequered and mysterious past emerged and these revelations soon went down in family history to be revived, re-told and re-polished when the family was gathered together. One time at Lurline Gardens in the late 1920s,

Nell answered a knock at the door to an imposing-looking woman with a sun-kissed complexion.

'I'm looking for Tom Bradshaw,' she announced. 'I'm told this is his sister's house and he often stays here.'

'And who wants 'im?'

'Mrs Vera Bradshaw née Swann. His wife.'

You could have knocked Nell down with a feather, but she thought on her feet, figuring that if Tom had a wife that he would be pleased to see he might have mentioned her. ''E ain't 'ere. Last I 'eard 'e was in India.'

'No, I'm afraid that India is one place he is not. Are you his sister?'

'Yes, I'm Nell Knight.'

'Well, Nell, pleased to meet you. Your brother often speaks of you. Tom married me in India and became a father to my three children. I was a widow. Two years ago, he said he was popping home to see his mother, who was ailing, and I've not seen or heard from him since. I think I deserve an explanation, don't you?'

'I think you do. I'd like to 'elp you. Really would. Tom walked out of 'ere more than 20 year ago and we've barely seen 'im since. 'E turns up once in a blue moon like the prodigal son.'

Mrs Thomas Bradshaw, formerly of India, seemed satisfied with Nell's answers and added, 'If you see him, tell him there's three children who don't understand why their stepdaddy deserted them.'

When Nell related the story to Tom with a casual, 'Your wife turned up 'ere yesterday', he shrugged.

'What? 'Ere?'

'Yes, 'ere, as large as life. Says you left 'er and three kids high and dry.'

'They're not my kids. I don't owe her any money and I don't want to see any of them again. The woman's a menace.'

Another time, Tom came into the house trembling, the blood having left his face, rendering him ghostly. It was not often anyone saw Tom under pressure, let alone terrified.

'You're not going to believe this, Nell, but I nearly got shot just now.'

'Shot? Shot with a gun? Get off with you. I don't believe you.'

'No, honest, on our muvver's deathbed. Two men comes up behind me on Oxford Street and stuck a gun in me back.'

'Did they rob you?'

'No, they marched me to a Catholic church and made me swear I'd never visit Ireland again in my life.'

'I didn't know you ever 'ad.'

'I lived there for a while a few years back.'

'Don't tell me, Tom, you left a wife and kids there and these men were her brothers.'

Tom laughed, but then explained that was far from the case. The two men were IRA, he said, and somehow they knew that Tom had served with the Black and Tans in Ireland. The Black and Tans was a motley army of men, to say the least, recruited on the streets of Britain from 1919 to aid the Royal Ulster Constabulary in Ireland. The RUC were on the front line at the time in the British Government's battle with those Irish people fighting for Home Rule. The offer of ten bob a day was a hard one to resist for war veterans, many of whom were struggling to resettle at home and to earn a living. However, Tom, having managed to live from 1914 to 1918 in the few corners of the world not to have been affected by conflict, did not have this excuse.

''Ow could you go out there and fight Irishmen? You're 'alf Irish yourself, you daft bugger,' Nell challenged.

'A quarter,' corrected Tom.

Unfortunately, Sam did not have the resource or guile of his older brother and he became an early casualty of the gathering

Depression. The Crucible Works had laid him off years ago and he was forced to present himself at docks, building sites and factories looking for a day's work where he could. Because of his physical frailty and his unwillingness to push to the front, he was rarely among the brawn selected. His nephew, Bill's Bill, would alert him to new ships arriving on the river so he could be one of the first to present themselves for loading and unloading but, even then, he increasingly found himself turned away. His day eventually turned into a predictable and pathetic routine: the labour exchange in the morning, drinking tea at the coffee stall at the entrance to Battersea Park on Battersea Bridge Road and running errands for the stallholder in the afternoon, then across the road to spend some time with Nell before returning home empty-handed and empty-pocketed to May and the kids. One of Harry Knight's earliest poignant memories was watching his Uncle Sam drinking the water that Nell had strained from the vegetables straight from the saucepan. In the poorer parts of London, the collapsing economy had reduced life to the level of survival of the fittest and Sam had fallen by the wayside.

Little had been heard of Teddy since he left to see the country and take its temperature, though through a series of postcards and letters Nell had got an idea of how his life was developing. To begin with, they were frequent and could sometimes run to several pages. He described life in Yorkshire among the mineworkers and in Nottingham, where he worked in the textile industry. He had seemed happy in Cornwall for a while, working in the tin mines, and mentioned a lady, but eventually he moved on. He was greatly enthused by the General Strike of 1926, but after that collapsed and the revolution did not materialise, his language was less strident. The letters became infrequent. In one he confessed to tramping from 'spike to spike', although he claimed this was to illuminate his social experience rather than through necessity. The spike was the workhouse and the law dictated that, unless a person became an inmate, he could only spend twelve hours inside, therefore Teddy would have had to work for four hours before or after his eight-hour sleep and meal. Then it was a 14-mile trek to the next spike to repeat the process. A small army of proud but down-on-their-luck ex-servicemen, the mentally ill and penniless souls were kept on a treadmill of traversing the country like a sad Circle Line of poverty and desperation. Teddy had now boarded the train.

As the family fortunes worsened, mirroring those of the country, nothing cheered people up more than a good murder, the more gruesome the better. The Knight boys were brought up on a diet of court proceedings read from the newspaper by their mother rather than Hans Christian Andersen or nursery rhymes. Nell had always been captivated by these stories and would tell her sons about many of the famous murderers who had prowled the streets before either of them had been born.

The name Dr Crippen was made for a killer and the case had caught the imagination like few others did, filling up pages and pages of news for weeks. The fact he had murdered his wife, then tried to escape by boat with his mistress dressed up as a boy whilst being pursued by Scotland Yard made it all the more delicious. And though the passage of time had consigned the case of Jack the Ripper to history, it was nonetheless still fascinating. As Nell delighted in pointing out to her young boys, the slaying of those East End prostitutes took place in the year of her birth and Jack the Ripper was most likely still alive.

''E could be anywhere. 'E could be living next door,' she'd helpfully observe.

However, Dr Cream was Nell's all-time favourite murderer because he had lived close by in Lambeth Palace Road.

'I must have met 'im,' she would reflect, although she would rarely have had cause to go anywhere near Lambeth Palace Road when she was three years old. He infamously went out into the night, offering prostitutes pills to improve their complexions and then watched as they died of strychnine poisoning.

Yet when murder touched the family, it was not seen as entertainment at all; in fact, the Bradshaws, the Knights, even the Melchiors felt stained by it for ever, even though the connection was slight. It was erased from the collective oral family history and buried as quickly and as deeply as possible – as evidenced by the cropped photograph of Sam's wedding day that stood on Nell's mantelpiece, all traces of Tichy Thorogood having been diligently destroyed.

The first Nell heard of the case was in 1927, after a young policeman had been found dead in a peaceful Essex village early one morning by the local postman. It was a truly shocking business and was plastered all over the front pages every day. Murder was a rare occurrence in itself, but it was almost unheard of for a policeman on the beat to be slaughtered. But it was the grotesque imagery of the reports that captured the imagination and horrified in equal measure. The young PC was found in a sitting position against the bank of a small country road with his pencil in one hand and his notebook lying next to him on the grass. He had been shot four times in the head and two of the bullets had shot the man's eyes clean out of their sockets. A stolen car associated with the murderer or murderers was found dumped in Stockwell but after that the trail seemed to go cold and the media fuss died down. Early the following year, the papers were alive with the case again when it was revealed that two men, who owned a small garage business on St John's Hill, had been arrested in connection with the murder. One was an Irishman named Withers. The other was named as Frederick 'Tichy' Thorogood.

It's Murder

On absorbing the news, Nell sucked in a whistle, rolled up her newspaper and set off for the shop. ''Ave you 'eard, Maggs?'

''Eard what?'

'You know the terrible murder of that young constable? They've arrested Tichy for it.'

'What are you talking about, Nell? What terrible murder?'

'The perliceman who they found with his eyes shot out. Don't you read the newspapers?'

Maggs didn't. She genuinely had not heard of the murder, or if she had, hadn't taken it in with all the other things going on in her life. The last statement, however, sent a shiver down her spine and a conversation she'd had with Tichy years earlier leapt back into her mind. Nell explained some more and said that the other man had confessed to being at the scene of crime but was blaming Tichy for the murder. Tichy, in turn, was blaming his accomplice.

'Thank God our mother ain't 'ere to see this. The shame of it all. We 'ad a perlice killer in our 'ouse. Nearly in our family an' all. It's too much to take in. I should have wrung his neck that day in the Latchmere not just socked him one. It would 'ave saved a poor perliceman's life. Poor man 'ad a wife and a baby. We never said it to you, Maggs, but Mum always said 'e 'ad the eyes of a murderer. Thank the Lord you was away from 'im, 'orrible little bastard!'

Nell had to find a chair to sit on, such was her excitement, as Maggs tried to digest the news. The older sister considered only then that Maggs had been deeply in love with Tichy for many years and quietened down for a few seconds. Only a few. 'Mind you, 'e might not have pulled the trigger. Was problee his 'complice. The Irish fella. Those Irish are fond of a gun.'

''E pulled the trigger, for sure,' Maggs stated.

''Ow do you know that? I thought you 'adn't been following the case.'

'I ain't. But one day Tichy says to me – I remember it like yesterday – 'e says to me that if you kill someone, your face is printed on the dead man's eyeballs. I remember 'im saying it. 'E really believed it.'

'If 'e said that to you, gel, you must go straight to the perlice. That's evidence, that is. The Irishman is innocent then and you must save 'im from 'anging.'

'What? And stand in the box at the Old Bailey and send Tichy to the gallows? I won't do that. I couldn't do that.'

'They'll hang them both anyway,' interjected Charlie, who had just got back from his round and was hanging up his hat and coat. He knew all about the case. He also knew about Tichy and his wife's previous relationship with him.

Charlie was right. Whilst Withers admitted to being at the scene of the shooting after burgling a country house, he maintained it was all Tichy's doings. Tichy, for his part, claimed that he was not even in the car or in Essex that night, despite forensic evidence to the contrary. Implausibly, he claimed to have been at home in Battersea in bed alone.

The 31st of May 1928 was one of those days etched into Nell's memory, although it was one date she did not repeat in company. It was the day they hanged Tichy at Wandsworth Prison. The papers said that the precise time of his execution would be 11 a.m. The boys were at school and Maggs came over to the flat in Lurline Gardens. Nell took a dusty bottle of sherry from her kitchen cupboard and poured them a Christmas glass each and they both sat silently watching the clock move towards the eleventh hour. When it chimed, they simultaneously gulped back their sherry in one.

'Good riddance to bad rubbish,' said Nell. Maggs remained silent and Nell noticed her pressing down on her legs to stop them shaking.

XIV

The Widow and the Tramp

The news on Teddy, what there was of it, was not good. He had left Battersea in 1922 and now, eight years on, all contact had dried up. Nell could not understand why he had not been home to see them at all and had stopped sending postcards and letters. It was not as if there had been a fallout of any kind. When he had left, her boys had been babies; now, they were on their way to being teenagers and they couldn't really remember their youngest uncle. It was, therefore, a shock in 1930 when Ted Forward, who had grown up on Cringle Street and knew the Bradshaws well, bumped into Nell on Falcon Road and remarked casually, 'I saw your Teddy a year or so back.'

'What? Where?'

'Shanghai.'

'Shang-bleedin'-hai? What the 'ell is he doing there?' And, as an afterthought, 'Where is Shanghai?'

'China. I was there on shore leave and I walked into a bar with my pals and there he was, sitting on his own with nothing but a drink. Large as bleedin' life.'

'Are you sure it was him?'

'Teddy Bradshaw? I've known him since he was knee high to a grasshopper. I said to him, "Teddy Bradshaw from Sleaford Street, Battersea?" And he says, "Ted Forward from Cringle Street! I'll be jiggered." And we had a good old chat and a drink.'

'What's 'e doing there? What did 'e say?'

'He's in the Merchant Navy like meself. I think he said it was his first trip. He was sailing for England the next morning.'

'Did 'e ask about us? Did 'e say anything about the family? When 'e's coming home?'

'Sorry, Nell, he's a funny one, your Teddy. He never said much at all. Small world, though.'

'Did you tell him his mother died?' asked Nell.

'I didn't know she had, Nell. Sorry 'bout that.'

Nell had no doubt that Ted Forward was telling the truth, for what reason would he have to spin such a yarn? She was relieved that Teddy was alive and presumably well. Yet she was angry that he had not bothered to contact his family and let them know how he was. His behaviour baffled her because he knew how she felt about Tom's long periods of invisibility and how important the family was. Teddy was supposed to be the sensitive one.

More unsatisfactory news came from Sarah Lock a year later. Sarah was a Knight, a sister of Henry's who now lived in Sleaford Street with James Lock, a boyhood friend of brother Teddy's. She revealed that one evening a few weeks earlier Teddy had called at their door and gone to the Duchess of York with her husband. ''E looked terrible, Nell. 'Ad a long beard with spittle in it and there was 'oles in 'is shoes and 'is 'air all matted. And 'e ponged something rotten. 'E told my James 'e was living up north, but I think 'e's a down and out.'

The Widow and the Tramp

Sarah was talking to Nell about Teddy as if he was someone of vague interest who had lived many streets away, not her long-lost, much-loved brother. She felt like giving her a clip, talking about Teddy like that. It was news she didn't want to hear.

She sought out James Lock. He could not add very much except that Teddy had admitted to tramping and that he had stopped by on his way to King's Cross railway terminus, where he was taking a train to the north, claiming he had some work there. He had asked if Nell was still at Lurline Gardens and said he was going to take a walk down to see her but, as Nell knew, he never did. It could have been something to do with the fact that James told him his mother had died a few years earlier. James Lock said Teddy had gone very quiet when he told him that and had left soon after hearing the news.

The thought of that pained Nell terribly. Teddy was particularly close to his mother. It also upset her that her long-lost little brother had been standing in a pub 500 yards away from her and she hadn't known it; that he did not feel able to come and see her, and she could not understand why. Learning of his mother's death like that must have been a hard blow, but possibly not totally unexpected, yet he did not choose to share his grief with his family. When she told Tom about it, he was relaxed.

'Don't worry, Nell. Don't take it personal. If 'e's tramping, he don't want us to see 'im. That's all it is. 'E wants to come back when 'e's made something of 'imself. Mind you, there's not much chance of that these days.'

'Thanks for cheering me up, Tom.'

In a classic case of shooting the messenger, Nell never forgave Sarah Lock, her sister-in-law, for bringing her this bad news in the first place and barely ever spoke to her again. ''Oo does she think she is, going round tellin' everyone that our Teddy is a paraffin lamp? Bloody cheek of the woman!' The fact that it was true and that she had only told Nell cut no ice.

Nell could not dwell too much on Teddy's fate because times were becoming so desperate that every family, every person that Nell knew was fighting an ever harder battle just to feed themselves and their families. The news was dire wherever you looked. The Labour Government, in which so many had invested their hopes and ideals, had failed and an emergency National Government had been formed to preside over the world slump and its implications. The Stock Exchange in London had shut for some days to avoid a complete flight from stocks and shares. Unemployment was at nearly three million and hunger marches and demonstrations by those without work were the order of the day. There were full-scale riots outside Battersea Town Hall as the jobless men gathered to protest. Nell could not see against whom exactly they were protesting: Germany was on its knees, its currency worthless, its people idle; even America had suffered the much-talked-about (but little understood in Battersea) Wall Street Crash in 1929. Apparently, you couldn't walk around Manhattan for fear of a desperate flying businessman, who had thrown himself from the top floor of a skyscraper, landing on you. It seemed to be a trigger for the ills affecting the rest of the world. Nell did not enjoy reading the newspaper at this time because it seemed like bad news was everywhere you turned.

It was not as bad for Nell as it was for others. She did not have a fortune, paper or otherwise, to lose. She and the boys had few luxuries to cut back on and although she might lose one cleaning job, there was always another somewhere else. It did make her wonder how badly the people whose houses she cleaned were being affected by the Depression because although they confided in her that 'times were hard' and 'things are becoming tight', she could not see any noticeable changes being made to *their* lifestyles.

They still had the car, the trips to the theatre and the cocktail parties, though they tried to make you feel guilty about accepting a wage from them in exchange for your labour.

Nell bumped along the bottom almost blinkered in her mission to run her house and nourish her sons in every way she could. Harry was proving to be inquisitive and especially bright; indeed, in an echo of what teachers had said about brother Teddy years before, more than one schoolmaster had described him as 'gifted'. This time there was some evidence to support the claim because at age 11 Harry won a much-sought-after scholarship to attend the well-respected Salesian College in Surrey Lane, Battersea. He was the only boy from his class to do so and one of the few from the whole Dogs Home area. Nell saw this as a massive achievement for the Bradshaw/Knight clan and, to be fair, so did the rest of the family, although young Harry was forever being ribbed by his uncles and his friends about mortarboards and canes, and hearing references to Billy Bunter from the *Magnet* comics. For a while, he even suffered the nickname 'Prof'. Harry himself had mixed feelings. He was forever being coached about 'bettering yerself' and 'getting on in life', but when progress was made in that direction he felt some did not like it. It was an intangible thing, but it was there. Not jealousy; more like betrayal.

His mother attributed some of his early academic success to an event that occurred one Sunday morning after she had been cleaning the *Daily Express* offices on Fleet Street. At Ludgate Circus, she turned left instead of right and took a stroll down Farringdon Road, where she browsed the second-hand booksellers' wares and other stalls lining the roadside. Her eyes were drawn to a 20-volume set of red, beautifully bound encyclopedias entitled *Pictorial Knowledge*. Nell flicked through the pages and was bewitched by the detail and the accompanying black-and-white photographs and illustrations within.

''Ow much you asking for these, mate?' she growled at the seller, as if she already knew the answer was going to affront her.

'Five pounds to you, love.'

'Five pounds! I'm a widder, you know. Lost my 'usband in the war and trying to bring up two young 'uns. Five pounds is more money than I've ever seen. You should be ashamed of yerself!'

Nell pretended to be – or maybe genuinely was – offended and the bookseller seemed startled and a little ashamed of asking for a fiver. 'Do you really want them, love?'

'That's why I'm asking yer!'

'How much you looking to pay?'

'I've got 30 bob in my purse. Two weeks' wages from me cleaning job. That's all I can give. But you can tell the Lord you 'elped a war widder give 'er two boys an ejucation when you kneel down and say yer prayers. 'Ow much is that worth?'

The market trader smiled at this unusual customer's impudence. 'You'll pay all the 30 bob now? How will you get the books home?'

Nell looked around and spied an encrusted wheelbarrow set up against a wall in a nearby alley. 'In this,' and she began loading all 20 volumes into the barrow, paid the man and pushed on home with her heavy literary load, over Blackfriars Bridge, down Stamford Street, along the river and past Lambeth Palace and then down into Nine Elms Lane. By the time she arrived back at Lurline Gardens that sunny Sunday lunchtime sweat was dripping off her brow and her arms felt like lead. Nell maintained for the rest of her life it was the best 30 shillings she had ever spent.

Ted devoured *Pictorial Knowledge* almost as much as his brother did and shared the same thirst for knowledge and experience. He had a shorter attention span, though, and could not train his lively mind to listen to teachers or complete examination forms successfully. There was no question of him sitting for a scholarship – there was no question of him sitting at all for any period longer than a few minutes. With their imaginations fired by *Pictorial Knowledge* and the tales of far-off lands from Uncle Tom, the brothers' quest for new experiences soon transcended Battersea and its immediate environs. Not having access to money was a handicap, but once they both owned second-hand bicycles (another luxury provided against the odds by their hard-working and ingenious mother) they explored southern England. They thought nothing of riding 50 miles on a Sunday, perhaps to catch butterflies on the South Downs, or to get lost in The Lanes in Brighton, or watch the raft race at Rye. More often than not, they would get most of the way home by employing their Battersea guile and hanging on the backs of trucks and lorries along the main roads until the driver spotted them and shooed them off before they slipped and went under the wheels.

The boys, like most of the rest of the country, had become devotees of the cinema, first lapping up the silent comedy of Charlie Chaplin, born and raised up the road (according to Nell, she 'must 'ave met 'im'), Laurel and Hardy and especially Harold Lloyd. Lloyd was a bespectacled, bookish-looking hero who found himself in unlikely situations, such as hanging off the hands of Big Ben, but his appeal to the boys was that apparently he staged his own stunts.

When talking pictures arrived, the medium's hold over the population and the boys was complete and the stars of the films, although mainly American, became heroes and heroines like never before. Pictures of Paul Muni, complete with scar, staring from the page of a magazine in a still from *Scarface*, the biopic of gangster Al Capone, were taped to the wall next to Harry's bed, whilst Ted preferred the irreverent humour of W.C. Fields, or the glamour and sultry sexuality of Jean Harlow. Nell, however, could not see the attraction, and was a late and reluctant patron of Battersea and Clapham's picture houses. She called them 'bug houses', believing they were unhealthy, and crawling with cockroaches and the like. And, as in the air-raid shelters, she believed that couples were using the cover of darkness to indulge in sexual passion. She still could not understand why watching a film of people, whether they talked or not, could be preferable to them being there themselves and interacting with the audience. The passing of the music-hall age was something she never quite came to terms with and she would always harbour some resentment towards the film industry, especially when she saw yet another theatre being converted from an old music hall to a new Odeon or Ritzy cinema. The Clapham Grand itself became the Essoldo Cinema and eventually, to her disgust, a bingo hall.

* * *

Nell and Lady Ware had kept in contact by letter ever since Nell's impromptu visit to Norfolk. They shared family news and commented on the state of the country – the letters were never brief. But when Lady Ware announced she was to be in London to see to some family business and would drop in for a cup of tea with Nell if she liked, an atmosphere of near panic took over the Knight household. Nell cleaned and scrubbed the house for a week before, and even went next door and cleaned the front step and windows of Mrs Mitchell's house. The neighbours thought she had finally lost all of her marbles. She told her boys that they must wash and scrub up and be on their best behaviour, and ordered Tom and Sam not to call around on this specific Saturday. Lady Ware was coming and didn't everyone know it.

'Wear your school uniforms,' she instructed Harry and Ted.

'On a Saturday, Mum? This Lady lady will think we are bonkers.' Even Nell could see the logic in this and did not enforce that particular edict.

Their mother had not fully explained her unlikely connection with the British aristocracy, inadequately saying only that 'circumstances had brought them together many years ago'.

Lady Ware arrived on foot, having taken a tram from Clapham Junction, and not in a chauffeur-driven Rolls-Royce, as Nell had feared and hoped in equal measure. They drank tea from Nell's finest Crown Derby china whilst Harry and Ted sat on the divan (hands resting in their laps lest they start fidgeting – fidgeting being Nellspeak for picking noses) and chatted with the friendly old lady, who was nothing like what they were expecting. They had cringed when they watched their mother almost curtsy when she answered the door.

The old lady established some ground rules almost immediately by telling the boys to call her Rose. She admired a cased Red Admiral butterfly that Harry had mounted on the sideboard and that Nell had forgotten to hide. It was held in place inside the case by a rusty nail skewered through its body.

'What a lovely house you have and what a lovely area, so close to the park. I'd love to take a walk in the famous Battersea Park, perhaps, boys, you could show me around later,' she gushed genuinely.

'Queen Victoria loved the park,' said Nell, searching for common ground. 'When I was a gel, she'd come down in her coach and stop and talk to us children. Wonderful lady.' That was news to the boys.

Ted and Harry did walk around the park with Lady Ware whilst their mother probably cleaned the house again in their short absence. She was very relaxed, almost playful, demonstrating a sense of humour that appealed to them. At one point, she said that most teachers are basically children who are too scared to leave school and that resonated with them. When they got back to the house, she suggested they go off out rather than sit and listen to two ladies gassing.

Inside, Nell and Lady Ware resumed their conversation. Lady Ware praised Harry and Ted, and said they were a credit to Nell and her late husband. She said how much she admired her for bringing them up as a widow and how she could feel a happy house when she was in one. When it was time to go, the two women hugged one another and Nell insisted she travel on the tram with the old lady back to Clapham Junction, but Lady Ware would have none of it. 'I'm 75 years old, Nell, but I feel like I'm 20. It's stupid, isn't it? I have had a good life, but I get cross that I won't be able to see all the places I want to – all because my life will run out without my permission. Still, what can you do? Tell me, Nell, is there anywhere in the world you'd like to visit?'

'I'm 'appy 'ere in London. It's where I was born and it's 'ere I'll die. It's a wonderful place. Good people. Plenty of shops.'

'Surely there's a place somewhere that you've heard about or read about that you'd like to visit?'

Nell thought for several seconds before answering. 'Galway. Galway Bay in Ireland. That's where my gran'father came from. 'E said it was the most beautiful place on earth. Sometimes 'e used to cry just telling me about it.'

'You'll get there one day, Nell, I'm sure.'

At this point, the boys arrived back at the house and they happily escorted Lady Ware back to Clapham Junction. They had both really taken a liking to the old lady. Before she passed through the ticket office to the platforms, she pressed a crown into each of their palms and made them promise never to tell their mother.

'She's a remarkable woman, your mother. A remarkable woman. But she has some funny ideas. She might think that me giving you a little something will bring bad luck. So mum's the word.'

XV

A Phantom Funeral

It was the first Wednesday in June 1932. Derby Day. Nell woke up in the early hours of the morning feeling extraordinarily troubled. First of all she thought she'd had a nightmare, but the worry that had manifested itself in an upset stomach would not leave her, even after day had broken and she had poured a third cup of dark-brown tea from the pot. She woke the boys as usual for school, but they soon picked up on their mother's anxiety.

'What's the matter, Mum?' asked Ted.

'I'm not sure, boy. I couldn't sleep at all last night and I just cannot get your uncle Teddy out of my mind. I think something bad 'as 'appened or 'e is in trouble. I think 'e may fetch up 'ere today, I can feel it my bones. Good job it's Derby Day and I'm not working or I'd 'ave to take the day off and wait in.'

The boys exchanged a knowing glance. Their mother and their uncles and aunties were slaves to all sorts of superstitions, including the throwing of salt over shoulders, never stirring tea anticlockwise, a fear of black cats, not passing on the stairs and touching a sailor for good luck (although Bill had told them that sailors themselves probably started that one), but they had never known their mother to have any truck with psychic forces. She had stopped reading Sir Arthur Conan Doyle's Sherlock Holmes stories when she discovered he was a spiritualist and attended seances. 'Can't take the silly sod seriously now,' she had complained.

Nell had also been highly disdainful about the furore surrounding an alleged ghost in a house on Eland Road, where she used to live. She knew the family concerned and had no time for their claims of a poltergeist, moving objects and smashing windows, which they said was blighting their lives. They even had the press crawling over the area for a few weeks. Nell said Mary Flynn told her that it was local boys running around and the whole thing was poppycock. 'Thank God we've upped sticks from Eland Road. I couldn't take the shame,' she pontificated.

Uncle Teddy was a mysterious and anonymous figure to the boys, having left home before he could register in their consciousness. They sort of knew he was probably a tramp, although nobody actually confirmed this to them. The nearest Nell got to acknowledging her brother's true state of affairs was to say that Teddy 'liked the outdoor life'. They were looking forward to meeting him again because, unlike Baby Henry, he was talked about often and openly, and his return was apparently imminent. Harry felt a particular connection because he was constantly told how like his uncle Teddy he was and how much they were going to get along when he came home. Nell also shared Teddy's old letters with her oldest son and he could see that his uncle was a thoughtful, articulate man with an acute social conscience.

Nell was genuinely surprised that by midday on that Wednesday neither Teddy, nor news of Teddy, had arrived. By now, her feelings of despair had intensified and she began to sob, not knowing what she could do. She understood the whole thing was irrational and tried hard to pull herself together before the boys came in early from school. Because it was Derby Day, they'd be let out at 1 p.m. But Teddy's face filled her mind, like a canvas in front of her that she could not turn away from. She recalled bathing him as a baby, walking him in the park and holding his little hand. She thought about how she and her mother fretted over his quiet ways, and she groaned as she considered, possibly for the first time, how the war and whatever he had done and seen had damaged him. She wondered if they all could have tried a bit more to help the angry and unhappy young man that returned from the carnage.

The boys had obviously forgotten about their mother's strange mood when they left school that day because neither of them came straight home. Harry would have lingered in the park on his walk home from Salesian College, as he often did, and Ted could have been anywhere. He'd be with his gang of chums and they'd be making their own amusement over at the goods yard on Stewarts Lane or maybe pestering the fishermen up on the ponds on Clapham Common. Harry was the first to come home at around 5 p.m. He set his homework out on the dinner table and immersed himself in his study. Ted arrived much later; having spotted his uncle Sam standing at the coffee stall at the entrance to the park, he had wandered over to chat to him. Sam was holding a coffee in both hands, as if he needed to warm his hands on the cup. Winter habits die hard. He wore his army greatcoat and a flat cap, a wafer-thin roll-up protruding from the black slit of his mouth, which was surrounded by two or three days of stubble. This was his normal garb come rain or shine.

'No Derby this year, Uncle Sam?'

'I ain't been to Epsom since '27, young Ted. I might raise the

fare there, but unless I win I might not get 'ome. Don't think
May'll be too pleased and don't fancy the walk, boy.'

Gino, the Italian man who ran the stall, was studying the
evening paper's back page, where the latest classified racing results
had been stamped.

'Who won it, Gino?' Ted asked.

'April the Fifth. Led from the off. You could of got 100–6 about
it. Fred Lane rode it.'

Ted shrugged, he had never heard of the horse or the jockey.

'Where you bin?' demanded Nell, as Ted sauntered in and sat
down next to his brother at the table. He realised that she was still
in a vexed state.

'I've been over at the coffee stall with Uncle Sam.'

'What? For five bleedin' hours? You brought in an evening
paper?'

'No, I ain't been near the shops. You want me to go and get
one?'

'I wondered 'oo won the Derby, that's all.'

'An 'orse called April the Fifth, Gino told me.'

Nell's head jerked up as she stood over the table cutting bread.
'What did you say?'

'April the Fifth. Fred someone rode it. It was an outsider. Pity
we—'

Nell dropped the knife and slumped back into her chair,
emitting a strangulated wail as she did so. The boys had never seen
her cry, let alone scream. It frightened the life out of them. 'Mum,
what's the matter? What's up?'

'I knew it. I bloody knew it. 'E's dead. 'E died today. Poor
Teddy. Gawd 'as just told me. Poor baby Teddy. I knew it, I did.
That's Teddy's birthday, April the 5th. April the 5th 1896. Gawd
'as just told me. You best fetch Sam, if 'e's still over there. Poor
wretch. He ain't died well, I know that. He ain't had a good death,

poor soul. And 'ow can we lay 'im to rest when we don't know where 'e is? Gawd tells us this, but 'E don't tell us no more.'

'Mum, he probably isn't dead,' Harry reasoned. 'Your hunch could be wrong. Don't get so upset, please.'

But Nell could not contain her emotions, even though she could see that the boys were upset and not a little scared by her loss of control. 'I don't unnerstand it. I don't. It's a bloody curse on my family, it is. My muvver, my farver, my 'usband, my little 'Enry and now my Teddy. When does it end, eh? I fought it had stopped when I gave the watch back to Lady Ware. She tried to give me money and I wouldn't take it. I says to her, "No! It ends here." But it 'asn't, 'as it? I don't want no bloody reward money. Neither did Mother.'

The boys looked at each other, concerned. Helpless. It sounded like their mother was rambling. Lady Ware, watches, rewards. What was she on about? Was she going insane in front of them? If she had to go into an asylum, who would care for them? What was happening? They needed help, but as they fled out of the door a deep sense of unease settled on them. The strange remark about refusing Lady Ware's money resonated as they silently recalled happily taking the benevolent old lady's five shillings each and spending it wantonly, being careful to keep the secret from their mother. Something they couldn't identify made them feel implicated and responsible for the surreal chain of events that were unfolding.

There was no comforting or reasoning with Nell and one by one the family turned up to witness her grief, all of them fetched by the panicking boys. By mid-evening the little flat was full: Bill and Dolly, Sam and May, Tom, Maggs and Charlie all trying to make some sense of what was happening. Only Sam went along with his sister unconditionally. He sat in the chair crying intermittently, using his grubby old scarf to wipe his face. 'Poor Teddy,' he echoed.

Whether his emotion was triggered by his belief that he had just lost a brother, or just because he was upset seeing his sister, who he idolised, so bereft was hard to tell. It was difficult for the family to accept, let alone grieve for their brother's death on the basis that their sister felt it and that the name of the Derby winner being Teddy's birth date was proof from above. If it were anyone else but Nell, they would have said not to be so ridiculous. Yet she was not given to hysterics or idle musings. Nobody doubted that *she* was utterly convinced that their brother had died that day; the problem was they were not.

Nell was sure that some physical proof like a letter from a workhouse, or a telegram from the police or a hospital, would arrive over the coming days and that any doubts her siblings had would soon be banished but no such confirmation was forthcoming. By the following week, she was strong and calm again but resolute in her belief. She announced to her boys, 'I don't know where your uncle Teddy is, p'raps we will never know, but just because we don't know doesn't mean we can't send him off in the way we should. We'll 'ave the funeral Saturday.'

Harry and Ted set off with heavy hearts to tell the family that a wake was being held on Saturday, first at Lurline Gardens and then down at the Cricketeers public house, for their lost uncle.

'She's not serious?' gasped Tom. 'We can't have a funeral or a wake for someone we *think* is dead – or someone your mum thinks is dead, more like. This is going too far. If people find out, they'll think us Bradshaws 'ave gone stark staring mad. They'll send her to Bedlam, if she ain't careful.'

'Are you coming or not then, Uncle Tom?'

'What time?'

Bill's reaction was similar. 'She's not still on that, surely? She wants a funeral without a body? I ain't never 'eard anything like it in my life. Do you hear this, Dolly? That sister of mine wants a

funeral for our Teddy because 'e's missing presumed dead – but only
by Nell. Well, I'll be blowed. What time does she want us round?'

Nobody had the courage to say to Nell what they were really
thinking and on Saturday afternoon they all turned up at Lurline
Gardens as agreed dressed in funeral black, although Tom and Bill
were both seen furtively putting on their black armbands just
before entering the front door. Nell had opened the sherry and
made some sandwiches, and she asked Bill, as head of the family
in age if nothing else, to say a few words. He was brief and
noticeably embarrassed.

'Well, looks like we're 'ere to send off our Teddy. It seems that
'e's gorn to join Baby 'Enry in 'eaven. 'E's a good lad and we'll all
miss 'im. Until we meet again!' Bill raised his glass and everyone
followed suit. Nell dabbed at her eyes with a handkerchief. Tom
fixed his eyes on the floor and Sam looked confused as ever. Harry
and Ted deliberately avoided catching one another's glance lest
they collapse into a fit of giggles.

In the Cricketeers, the mood lightened as the drinks flowed and
Nell seemed to relax now she felt she had done right by her
brother. Everybody else just hoped that nobody who knew the
family too well would come in and ask whose wake it was.

Sod's law prevailed, though, and in walked Ted Forward from
Cringle Street with his wife and her brothers – the Ted Forward
who had bumped into Teddy in the Shanghai bar years before.

'Who you buried today then, Tom?' he asked, looking up and
down at the black suit and the armband.

'We've 'ad news of our Teddy's passing, I'm afraid,' said Tom,
pleased with his quick answer because it was sort of true.

'Blow me down, Tom, I'm sorry to hear that. He's only my age.
What took him off then?'

'The consumption,' Tom answered without a flicker of
hesitation, and he looked to Bill to ensure he had heard and did

not give a conflicting explanation to anyone that may have asked.

'The consumption,' Bill nodded solemnly in agreement.

'He was on the road, wasn't he, your Teddy? No wonder he caught the consumption. Where was he when he died?'

'Liverpool.' This time it was Bill who provided a quick answer.

'Yeah, Liverpool. He was buried up there before we 'eard about it, so we are 'aving a wake for him today,' Tom added, getting into the swing of fabricating his brother's demise. Ted Forward wandered off to the bar, having no reason to doubt anything, feeling only sympathy for the Bradshaw family

Tom then turned to Bill and whispered out of the side of his mouth, 'You know what, Bill? The worst thing that could 'appen now is for our Teddy to walk through that door.' The vision sent the two middle-aged brothers into fits of childish laughter that were only controlled when they felt Nell's eyes piercing them from the other side of the bar.

XVI

Weighed Down

By 1934, the two shops Charlie and Maggs owned were in jeopardy. The Hill, as the shop on St John's Hill was commonly referred to, was just washing its face but the Wandsworth Road store was losing money. Sid Harris, a school chum of Charlie's, now ran Wandsworth Road whilst Maggs and Charlie looked after The Hill. In reality, it was Maggs that ran the shop, as Charlie spent most of the day buying the produce and then went off out on his delivery round until mid-afternoon. Maggs had serious doubts about Sid and believed that much-needed takings were slipping through the till and into his trouser pockets.

'How could you think such a thing?' protested Charlie. 'Sid's one of us, he grew up with me on Cedars Road and worked for Dad before me. Maggs, he's a Battersea boy, for heaven's sake.'

''E's a Battersea boy': that summed up Charlie, thought Maggs. She cursed this blind trust and the affection he had for everyone who happened to share his streets and his past. The trouble with

Charlie, she often rebuked him, was that he only saw the good in people. It was a common occurrence at The Hill to see Maggs taking Charlie by the arm and guiding him outside, then point to an individual nearby.

'Who is that, Charlie, coming down from the Plough, half sozzled?'

Charlie squinted.

'I'll tell you 'oo it is, Charlie, it's Mrs Spall, that's 'oo it is. The same Mrs Spall who you let off settling her tick this morning and will still give a sack of spuds. But she's got enough money to fill 'er belly with stout!'

'She always pays in the end, Maggs.'

'There is no end, Charlie,' sighed Maggs exasperated.

Charlie sighed too because he knew he would not put any pressure on Mrs Spall until her husband, George, was back in work.

Charlie loved his delivery round more than anything. Rolling his van down the East Hill and out onto the Portsmouth Road, he felt free of the worries of being in business and surviving in a country that was on its knees. There was no Maggs watching over him. No customers asking for credit. He was on his own and he stretched out this tranquil time as long as he could. It was not meant to be like this. When Dad was around, he looked after the money side and there was always more coming in than there was going out. Now, it seemed as if it was the other way round. It was. Even the deliveries were suffering, with customers closing their orders and Charlie having to drive further afield to replace the lost ones. He now drove as far out as Reigate in Surrey, where the ravages of the Depression had not yet impacted on the big country houses and leafy streets. Still, this cannot go on for ever, surely? he thought. Things had to start getting better eventually.

Maggs wanted him to knock the round on the head, but

Charlie had so far persuaded her that as soon as people had money in their pockets again it would be highly lucrative and pick up fast. Delivering the produce was the future – he was sure of that. To abandon the core customers now would be suicide. His first stop each morning was by the windmill on Wimbledon Common, where he opened up his sandwich box and had his lunch. Sometimes he'd sit for an hour watching the nannies pass with their infant charges, some clutching wooden yachts to sail on the ponds. Then, if he knew there was time, and there normally was, he'd venture over into Richmond Park and observe the deer, fascinated that herds of these beautiful, serene wild mammals could be grazing just a few miles from his house and mucky, industrial Battersea.

'Charlie, we've got no choice. We've got to close Wandsworth Road down. It's bleeding money from The Hill. It'll be the death of us if we don't.' Maggs had made the decision and Charlie knew in his heart she was right, but he was always hoping against hope.

'What about Sid?' he asked plaintively.

'What about Sid? What about us? What about our kids, Charlie? Who would you rather feed first: Charlie Boy, Violet, Mary and Nell or Sid Harris and his tribe?'

It was a question Charlie could not bear to contemplate. Clearing the shop and putting up a sign saying 'CLOSED DOWN' rather than simply 'CLOSED' pained Charlie terribly. This had been the Melchiors' first shop, started by his grandfather, the son of a German immigrant, but worse than the pain of seeing the family business falter for the first time and under his stewardship was having to let go of Sid Harris, his old mate. Sid was all right whatever Maggs said. Mixing with the likes of Tichy Thorogood had made his wife see the worst in people. Many years earlier, as kids up on Clapham Common, some wide boys from Kennington had started to push them around and ducked Charlie under the fountain. Sid had stepped forward and whacked the main offender in the stomach, doubling him up in the process. 'Run, Charlie, run!' Sid had shouted, and the two boys had scarpered like billy-o before the bullies could retaliate. Charlie never forgot things like that. Later, Sid spent a few months in approved school for pinching the baker's moneybag but that was the only trouble he ever got in. Charlie had made the mistake of mentioning this to Maggs once.

'You're sorry, Charlie? I'm bleeding sorry. 'Ow bout you come 'ome with me and tell my missus 'ow sorry you are? 'Oo wears the trousers in your 'ouse, Charlie? Maggs says this and Maggs says that. Ain't you got a mind of your own? I never thought it of you, Charlie. Your father will be spinning in his grave, Charlie, if he sees what you are doin'. Where d'you think I'm going to get work now? I ain't, am I?'

Sid's reaction shocked Charlie. He had thought a family friend would be more understanding of the situation and maybe would have shown some gratitude for the years of employment the family had given him. But people don't always work like that – even Battersea boys. Charlie felt worse about Sid than the traumas looming ahead for him and his own family, and for Maggs that was his abiding character flaw.

When Maggs finally announced the round had to go too, Charlie was devastated. She had calculated that the profit on the orders was barely covering the petrol used to travel the long distances. She said that it would make far more sense for Charlie to work in the shop full time and for her to get a little cleaning job in the mornings because Nell had assured her they were still about if you looked hard enough. The rest of the day, she would look after the kids. Nell thought this made perfect sense and was not backward in saying so. She always said that having the kids hanging around, looking dishevelled and hungry, was a poor advert for a shop selling food. Charlie tried to dissuade his wife but could not produce any credible argument to support not doing as she said. It was becoming harder and harder.

Bad luck, fear and hardship were hunting him in packs. The families from the big houses on the common were no longer sending their maids down for the daily or weekly shop. Perhaps they no longer had maids, or maybe they were swallowing their pride and they too were shopping at the market, where the fruit and veg were undoubtedly cheaper. Charlie tried to match their prices, but he could never go as low as the traders because they did not have the overheads of a premises. If he did, he would be selling produce at less than what he had paid and even he realised there was no future in that. Within pip-spitting distance, there was a market on the approach to Clapham Junction and another stall at Falcon Road making the competition fierce, and Maggs told him he had to get out into the street and shout the odds like the traders.

'We're shopkeepers not costermongers, Maggs.'

'Yes, Charlie, we are shopkeepers. Desperate ones.'

Charlie's descent into serious depression could possibly be traced back to the day he was forced out onto the pavement to plead with the public to buy his perishables. He was never a shy man, but he had his dignity and never thought he would be reduced to pushing cauliflowers into people's faces. Mercifully, he could not see then that far worse was to come.

Despite having a brood of his own, Charlie continued to take out Nell's boys right into their teens. Sensitive to them not having a father, he had always done more than the average uncle to help out Nell and provide an adult male presence in their lives. He had a good relationship with them and they all looked forward to Sunday mornings, when Charlie's van offered them endless opportunities for days out. Charlie and Ted shared a longing for the countryside and they travelled as far as Box Hill and Frensham Ponds in search of butterflies and birds and their eggs. Charlie and Ted would shin up a tree to raid a magpie's nest. Ted would clamber the last bit, where the branches became thinner, and Charlie would wait below him to catch him should he fall. One afternoon, they found a female bullfinch sitting on her eggs in a hedge. She did not fly away when Charlie pushed his hand into the gorse towards the nest. He gently lifted the bird off her brood whilst Ted deftly stole one of the eggs from the nest. 'That's the bravest bird I ever met,' declared Charlie. 'Put the egg back, eh, Ted, shall we?'

They fantasised about getting out of Battersea altogether, away from the soot of the Morgan Crucible factory and the smell of the candles from Prices, and into the crisp fresh air and their own little family smallholding, providing them with a living as well as their own eggs and poultry.

Harry, on the other hand, preferred the Sunday trips into London town, when they would stroll down the Embankment and watch the screevers at work as they drew with chalks and pastels to produce in minutes striking portraits and landscapes on the paving stones. One man could knock up a Mona Lisa in 20 minutes, which seemed, to Harry's untrained eye, to be every bit as good as Leonardo da Vinci's original. Another favourite haunt was Speakers' Corner in Hyde Park. This was always good entertainment, for here democracy worked at its most basic with an array of people attempting, but normally failing miserably, to attract a crowd and convince them of their argument, whatever that may have been. They saw them all: fascists and communists, warmongers and pacifists, religious zealots and lunatics, do-gooders and con men, end-is-nighers and out-of-work actors. Foreigners excited the crowd most and attracted extreme hostile reactions, for whatever the weaknesses and idiosyncrasies of the other speakers they were still English and therefore commanded a minimum level of respect and decorum. The foreigners, though, were fair game and absorbed most of the barracking. Those from the Orient in particular seemed to provoke hilarity in the crowds and Charlie was often the first to shout, 'Hurry up, my old China, we ain't got all day!' as a diminutive Asian man climbed onto his soapbox to address the crowd.

Charlie also owned a harmonica. He rarely played it, but he carried it in the breast pocket of his jacket everywhere he went. Other people kept combs or cigarettes in these pockets, but for Charlie it was his harmonica. At weddings, funerals and other family occasions, others would urge him to play and when Charlie blew a mournful 'Danny Boy', it never failed to bring a tear to the eyes of those gathered – their emotions having been already unlocked by Guinness and sherry. With the Bradshaws, there was a near-dormant volcano of Irishness that bubbled up involuntarily at times like these.

Ted remembers the time he lifted the harmonica from Charlie's jacket, as it hung over the back of the chair, when he was at the flat drinking coffee with Maggs and Nell. He leapt around the room making a din until his mother smacked him with the back of her hand, rather hard for his liking, around the head. 'Fetch that back now,' she ordered.

After Charlie and Maggs had left, Nell warned Ted, 'Don't ever play with other people's mouth organs, d'you understand?'

'Why, Mum?'

'Because they've been in other people's mouths and carry all sorts of germs.'

'It's only been in Charlie's mouth and 'e's my uncle, ain't he?'

''E is,' agreed Nell, pausing awhile before finishing, 'but he ain't a Bradshaw and he ain't a Knight. You 'ear me?' Her tone signalled that no further explanation would be forthcoming.

In hindsight, the family realised that Charlie's descent into despair began when The Hill was closed, although, in reality, he was already like a battered boxer, finding it harder and harder to get up as each blow rained down on him. Maggs had been telling him that the 'bleedin' books don't balance' for ages, but now there was not enough money to pay all of the rent on the shop and the landlord was losing patience. Meagre takings meant that there were fewer vegetables on display and they were more careworn-looking, and this in turn put off more customers. It was a vicious, predictable circle.

When there was no other choice and The Hill was finally shut in the winter of 1936, it was like a knife through Charlie's heart. He blamed himself that, for the first time in 60 years, there was no longer a Melchiors' shop in Battersea. His incompetence had destroyed the family business. He had done a disservice to his father and grandfather and also to his children. He felt utterly useless and powerless. Maggs told him that he should not reproach himself and pointed out that Sadie Hancock next door had closed down her milliner's and she was Jewish (by this, she meant Sadie knew how to run a business). But other than that, she did little to lift Charlie out of his all-consuming misery because she had the small matter of family survival to worry about.

Charlie withdrew inwards, trying to steel himself for whatever was coming next. Mentally, he had curled up into a ball with his knees drawn up to protect his testicles, his arms guarding his head from the kicking life was dishing out. Queuing and collecting the dole was another sickening milestone in his descent down life's greasy pole. Trying to find work and being continually rejected was another. He was now nearing 50 and, like his brother-in-law, Sam, he soon found that the most able-bodied and fleet-of-foot got what little work there was.

A sign of the times was groups of men standing on street

corners at all hours, smoking and talking, dressed uniformly in their caps and long coats and wearing their enforced idleness awkwardly. For a short time, Charlie found some work in a pub on Tottenham Court Road. But to save the sixpence bus fare each way, he walked to and from work and this, coupled with a lack of food, caused him to lose weight rapidly and he became gaunt and dishevelled. This probably led to his being let go by the publican.

At this point, Maggs made the decision that the family's best interests were served by her going to work full time and Charlie remaining at home, minding the children. 'That way we get your dole, whatever I can bring in and the kids are not left roaming around.'

Charlie could not demur. His demurring days were over.

On the night of 23 December 1936, Charlie called in alone at Nell's in Lurline Gardens. He, Tom and Nell sat and drank coffee whilst putting the world to rights. By this time, much to his mother's chagrin, Harry had left home. He had not stayed on at Salesian's to sit his matriculation and this mortified Nell. She saw this as his golden opportunity to break free of Battersea; it was a passport into another world – the world of 'getting on in life'. Instead, he had taken himself off to Gravesend in Kent and enrolled in the Merchant Navy training college before setting off on his first voyage. That night, Nell had no more idea where he was in the world than she did who would win the 3.30 at Alexandra Park the following day.

'It's your bleedin' fault,' she shot at brother Tom, who she held responsible for her son's wanderlust, 'filling 'is young 'ead with all those stories about foreign lands.'

Tom laughed, as he always did. 'No, Nell, it's your fault buying him all those bloody 'cyclopedias!'

Ted, though, remembers the evening of Charlie's visit just

before Christmas and that his mother and uncles had commented on the goings on in Germany and Spain, and the problems with bloody fascists. Charlie had turned to him at one juncture and said, 'I've got something for you, young Ted,' and passed him a small packet wrapped in brown paper and tied with string. It was his harmonica back in its original box.

'Doncha wan' it no more, Uncle Charlie?'

'I've got a new one, Ted. You should see it, she's a beauty.'

Charlie left shortly afterwards, and mother and son both agreed that he had not appeared so cheerful in a long while. He seemed to have come to terms with things and was not hanging his head in despair. There was a strength and resolution about him. 'And you can throw that blimmin' mouth organ away too,' Nell huffed as she lifted her eiderdown and stepped into her bed.

Back at his home later that night, Charlie told Maggs he had heard about a job as a porter going down at the old soldiers' hospital in Roehampton and he was going to rise early to be the first in line to apply. Maggs expressed doubt that a porter's wage could be more than the dole and the price of her giving up her little cleaning jobs.

'Let's see what it pays first, doll,' said Charlie, and Maggs was pleased he seemed to be fighting back a bit at last. His alarm clock was set for 4.45 a.m., which Maggs thought was taking keenness too far. He left a half-drunk cup of coffee on the kitchen table and set off in the opposite direction from Roehampton around 5 a.m. Somewhere between his house on Wandsworth Road and Vauxhall Bridge, he collected ten heavy iron horseshoes and put five in each of his greatcoat's side pockets. At 5.25, a taxi driver had seen him in his headlights climbing up on the structure of Vauxhall Bridge and jumping feet first into the Thames. The taxi driver told the inquest he was struck by the way Charlie kept his arms straight by his sides, as if standing to attention. It was still dark.

Charlie's suicide provoked more anger and shame in the family than it did sympathy. The law decreed that the act of suicide was a criminal offence, but by its very nature there was nobody left around to file charges against. You could not send a dead body to prison, although somebody had probably considered this. His funeral was dealt with quickly and quietly, and Charlie's fate soon became something that was not talked about. He joined Tichy Thorogood in the family's skeleton cupboard. Harry noted sparingly in his diary: 'Charlie did himself in today.'

Maggs was mad as hell and seemed anything but the grieving widow. 'The cowardly bastard,' she ranted. ''Ow could 'e do that to us? At Christmas time too. 'Ow could 'e do that to those poor children? 'Ow we gonna live, Nell? 'Ow we gonna live? 'E could 'ave at least warned me.' Which, of course, he couldn't have done.

Nell shared the view that Charlie had done a terrible thing and only in later years did her feelings toward him mellow when she better understood what he must have been going through. The poor children had no time to grieve and were conditioned to resent their father. Maggs instructed them to tell anyone who asked that their father had drowned, which was not strictly a lie. Maggs turned to Nell for support, emotional and practical, and she was only too ready to help. She saw the Melchiors as her equal responsibility now. Ted would often listen as the two women talked into the night, assuming he was asleep. They would speak with the gas turned down so as not wake him, and they only interrupted their conversation to slurp cocoa and puff cigarettes. For many months, the late-night conversation would turn to Charlie.

'I can't understand it, Nell. Things were bad, but they weren't that bad. None of us were starving to death or anything. What must he 'ave been thinking? And to think he planned it all out.'

'You know what I'd like to know?' Nell whispered. Ted strained his ears to find out what it was that his mother so wanted to know about his uncle's tragic death. 'I'd like to know where 'e got them bleedin' 'orseshoes.'

I'd like to know where 'e got them bleedin' 'orseshoes – this, from Nell, became Charlie's pathetic epitaph for the rest of his death whenever the family discussed his sad fate.

XVII

Goodbye, Brother

Nell helped Maggs move from Wandsworth Road to a house at the Dogs Home bridge end of Battersea on Wadhurst Road. Maggs and the children had the house to themselves and as the landlord was the local council, rather than one of the Scrooge-like figures who preyed on young families, it was sensitive to their predicament. Indeed, they were on a waiting list for one of the new homes being built under the slum-clearance programme, whereby the older houses of Sleaford Street, Thessaly Street, Savona Street and Wadhurst Road were steadily being razed to the ground. They were being replaced with modern flats fitted with all the mod cons, including indoor bathrooms and toilets, hot and cold water on tap, and gas and electricity. A world of relative luxury beckoned for all. For Nell, it was the location that mattered most because now Maggs, with her three girls and Charlie Boy, were close at hand, where she could keep an eye on them all.

With Harry still away at sea, and apparently relishing his life of travel and adventure, and with Ted now also at work – he had landed his first job as a messenger boy for the Twentieth Century Fox film company in the West End – Nell found that she could take her foot off the pedal. She decided to drop her two cleaning jobs during the day and retained only her early mornings at a doctor's surgery and a private house in Sloane Square, and her evenings at Lloyds Bank on Lombard Street. She was therefore free from 9 a.m. in the morning till 5 p.m., and so volunteered to take care of the Melchior children whilst their mother got herself a better job to replace the odd bits of cleaning she had cobbled together.

Although Maggs was now in her late 40s, she had retained her good looks and could always 'scrub up well'. Ironically, shortly after her husband had concluded that there was no light at the end of his tunnel of despair, things did start to look up. Unemployment had been falling, according to the Government, and now there was evidence everywhere. Work was popping up all over the place and people seemed to have that little bit more money to spend. There were more and more cars on the roads, the cinemas were packed most nights and companies were manufacturing consumer goods like radiograms, gramophones, telephones and vacuum cleaners. Slowly but surely, domestic items such as these trickled down the social scale.

One of the first jobs Maggs applied for was as a 'nippie' at the famous Lyons Corner Houses. Nippies were the young uniformed girls that flitted among the tables, taking and delivering orders from an enthusiastic public smitten with the concept of mobile food – dishes travelling along a Meccano-like factory-line system that traversed the restaurant – and American-style ice creams. Maggs had ignored the advert's stipulation that girls had to be 'young' and at her interview she was told she was too old to be a nippie. Yet the manager saw something in her and admired her spunk for trying. When he learnt that she had run two shops, he agreed to give her a trial as a trainee supervisor in their Charing Cross restaurant. His hunch was soon proved correct. Maggs showed a flair for running the team of young girls and became a permanent staff member within weeks, moving on to the busier Oxford Street branch. She loved the job and struck up a great relationship with the girls, who respected her for putting on her apron and getting stuck in serving at tables at the drop of a hat. She led by example, showing them she could be the fastest and most efficient nippie in the joint. She confided to Nell that her real reason for spending so much time at the tables was because she could garner so much in tips.

'Nell, no wonder this world is in such a mess,' she would laugh. 'It's because men run it, and men are so bleedin' stupid. All I need to do is smile and look in their eyes for a second or two and they're diving into their pockets to leave me tips. It's so easy to work the silly old buggers. Some of them ask me what time I finish after they've left me five bob on a saucer and I say, "I'm sorry, I'm a happily married widow," and turn around and scoot off.'

On top of her £2 5s 6d a week, Maggs claimed she could lift the same again in tips, far more than the younger girls. With the help of Nell, her life was looking up again and her sister assumed that it was only a matter of time before another man entered her life. Knowing Maggs, she'd capture a millionaire this time.

In 1938, a letter arrived at Lurline Gardens informing Nell that Lady Ware of Docking Hall had passed away. She had apparently reached the grand age of 83. Nell registered only then that she had not received a Christmas card from her the previous year. The letter was from Lady Ware's solicitors in Fakenham, Norfolk, and it asked Nell to make contact by telephone. She was immediately filled with foreboding, for she convinced herself that her friend had left her money in her will and she knew that she would have to forsake any bequest. Much as she was fond of Lady Ware, mention of her name stirred up all the emotions that still seethed inside about her father, her mother, the watch, and the reward and its attendant curse. She could not open that Pandora's box again under any circumstances.

Not having a telephone and never having visited a telephone box in her life, Nell asked Mrs Lowther, wife of the doctor she cleaned for in Sloane Square, whether it would be permitted to use their telephone if they stopped the cost from her wages. She was also quite thrilled to show Mrs Lowther the letter, which proved that she, a common charlady and washerwoman, had definite connections to the English rural aristocracy. Mrs Lowther was suitably baffled and very happy for Nell to use her telephone.

'Mrs Knight, thank you so much for ringing,' purred a voice at the other end with a country accent, yet with a hint of public school. 'I do hope you were not left in too much suspense, but I wanted to talk to you before we sent out a letter carrying out Lady Ware's wishes. I am Mr Teather, forgive me, Mr Teather of Teather and Sons, solicitors and commissioners of oaths. We are executors of Lady Ware's will. Lady Ware is your good friend, is she not? May I read out a small extract from Lady Ware's accompanying letter? The part that concerns your good self.'

Nell wished he would get to the point. 'Yes, please.'

'Off we go then. Now, where am I? Ah, yes, here it is. "I also wish that my dear friend, Mrs Ellen Knight, of 3 Lurline Gardens, Battersea, London, be assisted in her desire to visit Galway, Ireland, the home of her ancestors. Under no circumstances should Mrs Knight receive any bequest from this will, but the executors must facilitate for Mrs Knight and a friend or relative to travel to Ireland, receive good accommodation and a driver/escort throughout their stay, which will not exceed one week. The estate will meet all costs and all arrangements are to be handled by the executor." Well, Mrs Knight, that's us. We are the executors. It is incumbent on me to arrange your little trip. All you need to do is tell us when, and who will be accompanying you. Leave the rest to us.'

Lady Ware's kindness made Nell feel warm inside. She had to admire her memory, for she could not recall telling her friend about Galway, and she also admired her shrewdness. Nell could live with being 'assisted' to visit Ireland and that 'under no circumstances' was she to receive any bequest from the will. She thanked Mr Teather and told him she would be in touch shortly. She knew she would go. The timing was fortuitous, as the boys no longer needed looking after and she could take leave from both her jobs, not having done so for years. Ted was unable or did not want to accompany her, so she turned to Tom.

'Me? Go to Ireland? You're joking, gel. They'd shoot me before I even got off the boat!'

'Don't flatter yourself, Tom,' Nell replied.

His little scare years earlier still troubled him and he was not to be persuaded. In the end, she invited Annie Mitchell, from next door, even though Nell had always professed to not like her. She called her 'The Merry Widow' on account of her unsubstantiated belief she 'carried on' with various men – the fact that she was a widow and a free agent seeming to have escaped Nell. Annie Mitchell also had Irish ancestry and distant family in Cork, so Nell decided 'she best take the old gel', who was, in point of fact, two years younger than Nell. Annie could not believe her luck: she was being taken on an all-expenses-paid trip to Ireland and, as Nell had told her, there would be a driver at their disposal when they got there.

'You must 'ave come up on the pools or 'ad it orf on the 'orses then, Mrs Knight?' probed Annie.

'Never filled a coupon in my life and don't bet. No, this has been something I've been wanting to do for a long time, and I've been putting something by.'

Nell could lie barefaced with the best of them, but Annie Mitchell knew this could not be true. People like them – poor widows with children – did not put anything by. In matters of money, they were always *behind* the game, not ahead of it. Somehow, Mrs Knight had come into some money – but what a strange way to spend it. Then a buried, fuzzy memory surfaced. She could recall, vaguely, seeing Mrs Knight step out of a Rolls-Royce once. Or did she dream it?

The trip to Ireland was a huge success and a landmark in Nell's life. To her, it was a major personal and social achievement. Her grandpa had urged her to visit Galway, not thinking she ever would or could, and she had. They were based in a 'posh' hotel in Dublin, and Eddie, their escort, took them out on trips to Galway, Cork and Waterford, and to racing at Tramore, where Eddie even gave them money to stake on the horses. It was like a dream come true. As James Bradshaw had predicted, she fell in love with the beauty of the Irish countryside and was engulfed by the open friendliness of the people. In Galway, she found the little chapel where her grandfather had been baptised a century and more earlier, and a charming priest introduced himself and chatted to her.

'Well, Nell, let me tell you, this place is full of your relatives. Bradys and Morgans abound – below the ground and above it. I could take you into the street and introduce you to dozens. Your cousins are all around you, my dear.'

'Thank you, Father.'

She saw herself as part of a bigger picture for the first time. She felt an affinity with an island that had existed before only in her active imagination. Standing in the little church, she sensed something and knew that her grandpa was with her. She had done something that gave great peace and contentment to them both.

On the social side, she was the first female Battersea Bradshaw or Knight to travel abroad; most of the males had only done so through the call of war. She was also the first to stay in a real hotel, and she made sure everyone she could possibly think of knew it. For an entire week, Battersea general post office was showered with postcards and letters; even those with a most tenuous link to Nell received a bulletin. She wrote to her son Ted:

> My Dearest Ted,
> I am writing this at the writing desk of our hotel. I hope all is well and you are eating well. Tonight a man is playing the piano and me and Mrs Mitchell will go down and lisen after dinner. Tomorrow we visit Waterford and will stay the night in a hotel. Eddie my driver said to me that Mrs Mitchell reminds him of Old Mother Riley. Did I laugh. Hope Uncle Sam is behaving himself.
> See you Saturday.
> Fondest love,
> Mother

During the trip, Nell and Annie had begun to call each other by their Christian names, but as soon as they stepped back on Battersea ground it was back to Mrs Knight and Mrs Mitchell. Nell was quick to tell all who would listen on her return that the only downside to the holiday was Annie Mitchell's bad behaviour. Nell mainly complained about her eating habits ('too disgustin' to talk about'), her flirting with any man who happened to talk to them ('she's far too old for any of that, but do she know it? No, she bloody don't!') and her habit of 'dolling herself up'. The latter was the fault that incensed Nell most because it took her by surprise. She'd never seen Annie made up before and she feared her neighbour's generous application of eyeliner, rouge and lipstick was causing men to think they may both have been prostitutes. Unsurprisingly, Annie was shocked and upset when Nell told her this.

Nell thanked Lady Ware in her prayers for assisting her in this life-changing trip. She knew that without her help it would never have happened. But she was relieved that she had not been bequeathed a gift or any money in her will. That is how she rationalised Lady Ware's death and the Ireland trip in her mind. However, when she got home and was greeted with the news that brother Sam had been taken ill and was on his deathbed, she began to believe that the curse of the drowned boy and his watch had raised its ugly head again. There was no time to agonise, though, as she rushed to be with her ailing brother.

Sam had taken to his bed on the Tuesday and died a week later in the Anti-Vivi Hospital up the road from his house. He had developed a virulent strain of some bronchial infection. The doctors had mentioned bronchitis as one of the causes of death, but it was some time later on, while scrutinising Sam's death certificate, that Nell saw the word 'malnutrition' buried among a series of diversionary and unintelligible Latin words.

'Gawd help us all if a young man can die of starvation in this day and age. And they tell us that those days are gorn. Well, they ain't gorn round here,' mourned Nell. She believed the premature demise of her younger brother was a scandal and clung to this reason for his death forever after. She was convinced 'they' had murdered Sam. Who 'they' was, she never specified.

Besides the tragedy of Baby Henry – and putting to one side the fate of Teddy, for, whatever Nell believed, his death had not been proven – Sam was the first mature sibling to die. It affected Nell badly, and she rued his sad life for the rest of hers. She said she was never sure who got dealt the worst cards: Henry or Sam.

Malnutrition may have contributed to Sam's death, but it is unlikely it was the main cause. He had been afflicted with illness all his life, and looked pasty-faced and hollow-cheeked whatever his circumstances. It is true that he ate badly, and sparingly, but it was not always because of the lack of opportunity. The Salvationists dished out free pea soup at a stall not so far from the one that Sam stood outside every day drinking coffee, but he rarely visited it. Harry and Ted can both recall him drinking the green water, but they remember other times when Sam turned down the offer of some dinner and preferred to sit and watch them eat as he puffed away on a Player's cigarette. He was never without a fag – it's possible he smoked 60 a day – and he'd had a distinctive rasping cough for as far back as anyone could recall. The addiction to tobacco could have had as much to do with his death as his erratic eating habits. Although he was still a relatively young man at 46, it was not uncommon for Battersea men of Sam's generation not to attain the half-century, even if they had survived the war.

Sam knew he was dying and his family was around his bedside continually from the day he was taken into hospital. He was already a grandfather and his children, who had pushed beyond the boundaries of Battersea, were recalled to their father's deathbed. Bill, Dolly, Bill's Bill and their families, and Tom and Maggs, were all also in and out. But it was Nell he needed to see and his greatest fear was that he would die without having said goodbye to her.

Once she was back from Ireland, Nell took control of proceedings, as everyone knew she would, and Sam's wife May could not have been more relieved. It was Nell who consulted with the doctors and she would be the one to sort out May's widow's pension, along with all the other hoops the bereaved are expected to jump through at a time when they are least equipped to do so.

'So, what was Ireland like?' whispered Sam when Nell first sat down next to him and the rest of the family quietly walked off the ward.

'Lovely, Sam. You'd 'ave loved it. I saw the church where they baptised Grandpa. It was just like he used to tell us.'

'That's good, Nell. And 'ow are you?'

'I'm fine, but I could 'ave done wivout all this. We'll 'ave to get you out of 'ere and 'ome.'

'I'm not coming 'ome, Nell. 'E's called me, although why 'E wants a useless old sod like me, beats me.' Sam looked up to the ceiling, as if he was posing the question directly to God.

Nell stared into his eyes, which looked like small misty puddles, floating on the floor of his sockets, and then at his poor old nose. Ever since that murdering bastard Tichy Thorogood had smashed him, Sam's face had taken on a concave shape, as if the imprint of that vicious fist remained, thought Nell.

Suddenly, Sam's eyes filled with tears. He tried to get his words out between heavy and laboured breathing. It was like a water pipe bursting. 'I'm so sorry, Nell, so sorry . . . Did Mother ever forgive me for what 'appened to Baby 'Enry? . . . It was my fault. I know it . . . That's why they left each other, they couldn't live together after what 'appened to Baby 'Enry. I still see 'im, Nell. 'E looked at me to 'elp 'im and I couldn't . . . I could swim an' all, but I never tried, Nell. I stood there and watched as the river fetched him off . . . I'm scared, Nell. I'm scared when I see 'im up there. I wish it 'ad been me that drowned, not poor 'Enry.'

The events of 40 years ago flooded back into that room as raw as the day of the tragedy. Seeing Sam in such torment and distress made Nell almost want to walk out of that hospital and throw herself off Albert Bridge. She pulled her chair closer to him and rested her pursed lips on his sweated brow. 'You daft ha'p'orth, Samuel Bradshaw. You silly old fool, you. Mother never blamed you for Baby 'Enry. Whatever makes you say that? Mother loved you like anyfing. She just wasn't the one to say fings, was she? God rest her soul. And it wasn't your fault. You was a boy yerself. It was nobody's fault. God took 'im. We don't know why, do we? 'E do fings we can't understand. Why did 'E take all those millions of young men in the war? Blowed if I know. That's the bit it don't tell you in the bloody Bible. And I'll tell you something else, Sam Bradshaw, you ain't got nuffin' to be scared of. Nuffin' at all. Because when you get up there, they'll all be waiting for you. Muvver and Farver, and they'll be together and 'appy, and Teddy'll be there, but most of all there'll be Baby 'Enry and he'll be so excited to see you. 'E'll say, "Where you been, Sam? What took you so long?" It'll be lovely. So lovely.'

Nell's tears gave motion to Sam's sweat and it trickled down his face to join his own tears and form a stream that rolled off his cheeks and onto the pillow. Brother and sister cried unreservedly, stroking each other's faces.

'Thanks, Nell. Thank you for everything. You've always looked after me. You been so good to me.'

'Don't be so daft. You've looked after yerself. You should be proud. You've a good wife and you've raised a good 'elfy family. What more can a man do?'

When she lifted her head again Sam's eyes were closed, but there was a faint smile on his lips.

Sam was buried in an unmarked grave at Streatham Vale cemetery. Henry Knight is nearby and Charlie Melchior not far away. Nell had the cemetery make a note of the burial plot, but when she returned she found it difficult to remember exactly where her loved ones lay without consulting the staff. Because of this, she claimed, she never visited the graves of her husband or any of the other relatives who would later join him and Sam. 'What's the point?' she'd say. 'I could be standing over any old person's grave, couldn't I? And there's most likely another ten on top by now.'

It was something that the others found at odds with her fierce loyalty to her family. Despite the words she spoke to Sam, she was not so sure about an afterlife and declared there was too much going on while we were alive to worry about anything after your death. Nevertheless, she did think ahead: she had taken out an insurance policy in 1921 to cover her funeral expenses when she died. She could not bear the thought of leaving anyone out of pocket.

As they filed out of the cemetery to take the tram back up to Battersea, Tom put his arm around Nell. 'Cheer up, old gel, there's still plenty of us Bradshaws left.'

'That's right, Tom. But you should stop smoking them fags. It was that cough that killed Sam, nothing else.'

'It wasn't the coughing that killed him, it was the coffin they carried him off in,' Tom joked as he lit up a Senior Service. Nell could only shake her head at her brother's incorrigibility.

XVIII

Blitzed

Talk of war had been on everyone's lips for many months. A resurgent Germany led by Adolf Hitler was on the march, arriving in neighbouring countries every other month, it seemed. With memories still relatively fresh and the effects of the Great War still very much in evidence, British people did not wish to become embroiled, although many knew it was inevitable. Nell greatly feared the prospect, knowing that once the country was involved it would be no short haul – and that again soldiers would be laying down their lives in their thousands, possibly millions. Her Harry and Ted, as young men in their prime, would be among the first to be called upon. The implications of that sent shivers down her spine.

Things were looking up for the family and the war could not have come at a worse time. Harry was now a well-travelled young man and when last on leave had talked of coming home, settling down and working in an office. He said he was going to take evening classes to study economics and he hoped to go into 'business'. It all sounded very grand. Ted, still only 19, seemed to have had a dozen jobs already. They were mainly in the West End and he worked chiefly as a delivery boy, but on the side he and his pal Harry Cousins were dabbling in all sorts of get-rich-quick schemes that were bringing in bits of money and bags of experience. Nell was quietly confident, and relieved, that her boys were going to achieve the 'Holy Grail' of poor Battersea families – getting on in life. Now, she fretted that a war was going to put paid to all that.

Harry Cousins had been a friend of Ted's since their early teens. Nell thought of him as a lovable rogue and called him 'The Imp'. He lived over the river in Fulham in one of the small terraced houses near the gas works, and he and Ted had become pals after sitting next to each other in school. Harry had been expelled from his school near Townmead Road and had been banished over the Thames to Battersea – what crime he committed was never fully explained. Ted had never thought of himself as poor – his mother often talked about 'the poor' and she certainly never included herself in that group – and when he visited Harry's house, he realised they were positively rich compared to the Cousins family. Theirs was a two-up, two-down red-brick labourer's cottage with an outside toilet and washroom. Harry was one of fourteen children, and the cramped and dirty conditions made Ted heave when he first visited. The younger children used a bucket for a toilet and this was only taken to the outside lavatory when full to the brim. Children sat scattered all over the bare floor, eyes wide and sparsely clothed, waiting expectantly to be fed like fledglings in a nest. Harry, at 13, had been pushed out of that nest, during the day at least, and soon honed his skills in fending for himself and bringing home 'little somethings' for his siblings.

Ted and Harry hit it off well. Nell could see that the boy was undernourished and had the eyes of a child who had seen things he maybe should not have. He talked openly about pinching things and Nell tried to convince him that as a little boy he might be able to get away with this, but as a young man they'd lock him up. Money not being as tight as it once was and food more abundant, Nell made sure she gave Harry plenty of bread and jam, and the water and sherbet with which the kids made lemonade, to keep him from feeling the need to steal food.

The boys' first entrepreneurial venture together was making rosettes from cardboard and ribbons and selling them to the crowds on Saturdays outside the football grounds of Fulham and Chelsea. Some bore the names of the teams' star players of the time, such as Vic Woodley, the Chelsea goalkeeper. Crude as they were and coloured by chalks and pastels, there were plenty of takers at tuppence a throw, and Harry was able to furnish his parents with some much-needed cash.

When they were 15, both lads had become messenger boys in the West End, charging around London on bicycles, and had cheekily managed to get themselves employed by more than one company at a time without the other knowing. When they became stretched, they helped each other out with the deliveries. In 1939, they were close to setting up their own delivery business, as London companies sought to communicate with one another in a mode faster than the daily post and telegrams. The outbreak of war and their rapid enlistment into the army shattered those grand plans.

War was soon official. Germany invaded Poland in 1939 and for the first time the 1914–18 war was referred to as the First World War. Harry switched from the Merchant Navy to the Royal Navy and within weeks Nell was living with the knowledge and fear that her two sons were now a soldier and a sailor respectively and would be soon engaging with the enemy.

At first, life in Battersea continued much as before. Although shelters had been constructed in anticipation of bombing raids and plans had been made to evacuate women and children out of London, in the first year of the war no such attacks materialised. Nell continued with her two jobs at the beginning and end of each day and still kept an eye on Charlie Boy, Violet, Mary and little Nell while Maggs was at work. Maggs was going from strength to strength with Lyons: they were using her as a roving manageress, attending to the restaurants that were short of staff or where the nippies were in need of some hands-on leadership. Her wages were good and, with Nell's help, the children were enjoying a higher standard of living and some welcome stability. Maggs herself was the happiest Nell had seen her, enjoying her work and making many new friends outside Battersea – most of them men. Nell felt it was only a matter of time before her sister remarried.

Tom had long since yielded to his advancing years and had laid down his hod and embraced yet another career change. He had picked up on a harmless, legal and easy-to-execute scam. This involved attending race meetings in the south of England, identifying enthusiastic but naive punters and making their acquaintance. He would put each one on to a specific horse in an upcoming race, claiming some inside knowledge, and make the punter feel he was privileged to have been taken into Tom's confidence. Tom would then move on, parting with a smile and saying, 'When it wins, don't forget to give me a little drink.' He would then find more punters and put them on to the remaining horses in the race. When the race was run, he would have every horse covered and at the end of the race he would then seek out the punter to whom he had recommended the winning horse and present himself all smiles and backslapping. Nine times out of ten, the punter was only too pleased to see the man who had helped to make him a little bit richer and would reward him with a crisp note folded into his outside breast pocket. In racecourse slang, Tom was now a spieler. This little performance provided him with a small living and satisfied his need to keep occupied and get out and about.

Bill and Dolly were now grandparents, living at home without children for the first time in nearly 40 years. They remained in Battersea, but some of their children had moved further afield to the new council estates and flats that were springing up in places like Merton, Mitcham and Wallington. Bill's Bill remained the last Bradshaw to make his living from the Thames, although by now he had moored his barge and hung up his sweeps in exchange for an easier life in the engine room of Tower Bridge. All the family took great pride in the fact that he was one of the men responsible for opening and closing the famous bridge and ensuring that the red double-decker buses did not tumble into the drink.

Despite fresh memories of the huge loss of life in the previous conflict, no one really believed the war could be lost, despite seeing France succumb to German forces, Winston Churchill replace Stanley Baldwin as Prime Minister and the army being driven out of Norway. History has made much of the great British spirit and the determination of the people, but for the Bradshaws and Knights they remembered it more as an attitude of let's get on with it, get it over and done with, and get back to normal. Defeat was not an option, not due to some intangible national spirit but because theirs was a generation steeped in the Empire. They were conditioned to believe that Britain was impregnable and always in the right, and would therefore prevail, whatever frightening evidence to the contrary presented itself day by day. The British people drove their stakes deep into the moral high ground and waited for right to triumph over wrong, as undoubtedly it would. When the war came to east London in the early days of September 1940, the Blitz causing the loss of hundreds of lives, even then the frame of mind was not altered. The only wobble was after Dunkirk. Nell remembered that people did contemplate a German invasion for a short period and there was much grumbling and suspicion that the aristocracy, from the Royal Family downwards, would be only too ready to adhere to German rule. Fortunately, some rousing speeches from Mr Churchill allayed these fears and united the country once again. Back in Battersea, the locals knew that because of the power station, the railway yards and the surrounding industry, the Luftwaffe would be likely to bombard them next.

Within days, they did.

On Sunday, 10 September 1940, Nell, Maggs and the children enjoyed a good roast dinner of beef and potatoes. Although rationing was now in place, Maggs was regularly given good meat from a man who supplied the Corner Houses and had taken a shine to her. After dinner, they lit up their Weights and the children went out to the road to play.

'I don't 'alf worry, Maggs, about 'Arry Boy and Ted. Sometimes I can't sleep, thinking they might not come 'ome.'

'Of course they'll come 'ome, Nell. They'll be all right, I can feel it in my bones. I reckon we're in more danger than they are. Did you 'ear last night that three 'ouses up on Dorothy Road were completely flattened? Last two nights we've been down the shelter in Stewarts Lane, but Charlie Boy panics as soon as we get down there. 'E 'ates it.'

'I don't blame 'im. You wouldn't catch me going down there with all them people squashing up together. Not me. When the siren goes, I get under the kitchen table and read the paper.'

Maggs laughed at the mental image. 'That won't do you much good, Nell, if your house gets a direct hit.'

'If it's got your name on it, Maggs, it's got your name on it. There's nuffin' you can do.'

Around 6 p.m. the alarms sounded and Maggs called in the children. They started to debate as to whether to go to Clapham Common Underground or the Stewarts Lane public shelter. Charlie Boy began to tremble and his mother said they would stay in the house. 'If it's got our name on it, it's got our name on it,' she repeated.

Nell left the Melchiors' home on Wadhurst Road and walked back to Lurline Gardens. It was still the early days of air raids and people were gathering belongings and scurrying off to whichever shelter they would be using. Later in the war, attitudes became far more lackadaisical and people would stroll around, ignoring the hum of the low-flying aircraft. Nell looked up as the German planes soared overhead, knowing on their return that they would be expelling their deadly cargo all over the streets she knew. She never thought she'd see the day when the enemy was so tangibly in her midst. The planes flew so low she felt she could stand on tiptoe and touch them. A sense of vulnerability and helplessness swept over her. Little did she know, one of those very planes was carrying a bomb not with her name on it, but with the names of her sister and her family.

For most of the evening, Nell could hear the distant thudding of bombs crashing down and she wondered if the City was being targeted and whether there would be any offices left for her to clean if the war carried on. Before midnight, the action seemed to close in and more than once the house most certainly shook and she could smell fire. The sound of the raid was now deafening and for the first time Nell felt really scared and scrambled under the kitchen table. She did not take a book or a newspaper, instead she prayed and made her arms ache crossing herself. As the night progressed, the bombardment did not relent. There were either thousands of planes passing over, releasing their deadly loads, or they had chosen to fly around in circles over Battersea. She realised that night that she might die.

By the early hours, Nell's back was aching and she decided that if she was to die, it would be undignified to do so under the kitchen table, so she crawled into her bed, where she fell into a deep sleep with the noise of bombs, planes and anti-aircraft gunfire filling her senses.

It was midday when she awoke. She jumped out of bed, realising that she had missed her cleaning chores at Dr Lowther's. She had never been late or taken a day's absence, other than to give birth and for her trip to Ireland, from any of her jobs since she had started work when she was 14 and she was devastated. She dressed quickly and emerged into the street. The pall of dust and soot that hung in the air immediately choked her. The houses on either side seemed intact, but as she came out onto Battersea Park Road she looked up towards the Dogs Home and could see only crowds of people, clouds of dust and ambulances. A river of water from a fractured pipe lapped over her feet. Dr Lowther would have to wait.

Once she was under the Dogs Home bridge, she could see the devastation to her right: the houses and streets which had stood only hours earlier were now rubble. The area had been cordoned off and police, army and ambulance men waded through the wreckage looking for bodies and survivors. Items of furniture eerily stood here and there, the walls that once surrounded them having disappeared. Displaced residents, shocked at the loss of their homes but happy to be alive, wandered around aimlessly as Salvation Army volunteers and civic officials tried to direct them to halls, churches and schools. Many insisted on getting in among the wreckage to rescue belongings despite the risk of unexploded shells.

'This ain't the worst of it,' chattered a man next to Nell. 'You know what the Jerry bastards done? They sent down a land mine on a parachute and it's destroyed all the streets over there.

Thessaly, Mundella, Patmore, Wadhurst, Stockdale – they're all flattened. Thank the Lord most of us were in the shelters.'

Nell ran down Stewarts Road and could see that the Germans must have been aiming for the railway and the goods yards. There was devastation everywhere. Two policemen stopped her as she tried to enter Wadhurst Road.

'My sister lives at number 37.'

Nell could see that number 37 was not there. Nor was number thirty-anything.

'They didn't go to the shelter.' Panic rose up inside her. The policemen put their arms around Nell and led her away.

'I'm afraid we have recovered some bodies from number 37. I'm very sorry. You'll have to come with us.'

Nell was shown to a police car and the officer told the driver to take her to St Thomas' Hospital. They were unable to move off, though, because of a procession of large black cars coming towards them at a snail's pace. Crowds of photographers and other local people ran alongside the vehicles. They stopped at the junction of Ascalon Street and Mr Winston Churchill, the Prime Minister, stepped out of the first car and Herbert Morrison, Minister of Supply, emerged from the second. The police driver manoeuvred around them and Nell looked back out of the window at the surreal image of Mr Churchill, in trademark bow tie and bowler hat, being led down the streets of her childhood.

Nell was spared identifying the bodies of her sister and her nieces and nephew because Maggs's neighbours had already done this. Maggs and her three girls had all died instantly, it seemed, when the mine had obliterated many of the houses in Wadhurst Road. Amazingly, they were the only casualties in the street. Charlie Boy had survived and had been taken to Roehampton Hospital. He was badly burnt and they didn't expect him to survive. She was asked if she wanted to see the bodies but was warned it would be a very disturbing sight. Nell decided she could not and persuaded the policeman to take her to Roehampton, which he kindly did, and he also diverted to Sloane Square on the way so Nell could explain to the Lowthers why she had been absent. Mrs Lowther was horrified – horrified that Nell felt the need to come and tell them.

The utter tragedy of what had happened did not sink in until the following day. Nell, Tom and Bill sat in Lurline Gardens, crying into their tea and hugging each other. They silently remembered their sister and her children. There were no words at first.

Nell had been unable to see Charlie at Roehampton in the afternoon. The doctors told her he was being stabilised and asked her to return the next day. Back at the house, the whole family had now gathered: Bill and Dolly, Bill's Bill and his wife, Hannah, Sam's boy Ernie Bradshaw and Tom. They sat around the room sobbing, making tea and stilted, inane conversation. For Tom, Bill and Nell, the feeling that their generation of Bradshaws was fast disappearing was left unsaid. All of them, and a procession of neighbours and friends who arrived to express their sympathy and solidarity, looked at the floor and shook their heads at the thought of the children. Violet, Mary and Nell had their young lives ahead of them. Charlie Boy was all burnt up like a piece of firewood, hanging on to his life by a thread. They all took comfort from Nell's news that the police said they would have died instantly and not suffered.

'That's good.'

'That's a small mercy.'

'Poor mites. At least they never suffered.'

'Thank the Lord for that.'

Over and over.

Charlie Boy stabilised. When Nell finally got to see him, he was covered from head to toe in bandages, like Boris Karloff in *The Mummy*, with a small air gap left for his mouth and nostrils. The nurses told Nell he had been asking for his mother and sisters. The ward sister said it was up to Nell whether she told him what had happened or not, but the truth could make him lose his will to live. Nell knew she could not lie to him. He was ten years old and not stupid. If he was coherent and he asked, she'd have to tell him. The doctor explained that Charlie had suffered serious burns to his face and torso and that, although he should survive, he would be hospitalised for many months, possibly years. When she sat down next to him and spoke, Charlie made her job slightly easier. 'Are they dead, Aunt Nell?'

'Yes, Charlie Boy. But they never suffered.'

Charlie said nothing at first. The only reaction Nell could see was him licking his lips slowly. 'What, all of them?'

'Yes,' Nell cried, wishing she could hold him.

'It was my fault,' he gurgled, as tears that could not escape ran down into his throat. 'I wouldn't go to the shelter.'

'No, it's not your fault, Charlie Boy. I told your mum that I didn't go to the shelter as well. It's that bastard 'Itler's fault, nobody else's.'

'We were all so scared, Aunt Nell. It was awful. We thought we were going to die. We all got under the bed and I crawled out because I was scared. I don't remember anything else.'

'Don't think about it, Charlie Boy. You just concentrate on getting better.'

'Where am I going to live? Who's going to look after me?'

'With me. I am, you daft bugger! What d'you think? We'd put you in Dr Bloody Barnados? No, no, you're coming 'ome soon to live with me,' Nell replied without pause. There was nowhere else. There was nobody else.

A year later, Ted was home on leave. The air raids continued but none were as devastating as those first horrific nights in September 1940 for the people of Battersea. Since Maggs and the children had perished, Nell had bowed to common sense and made use of the public shelters or the Underground, although she still considered it a great nuisance and resented every second – Ted always said he would sometimes rather have taken his chances above ground than go down the Tube with his mother, such was her complaining and chatter throughout the night.

'You'd think they'd clean the bleedin' platforms before they expect people to sleep on 'em,' was a constant refrain. More embarrassing was her stern glare at any couples she suspected might be attempting to be so rude as to secretly copulate.

* * *

One morning in November 1941 mother and son emerged from the Clapham Common Underground station and began walking back to Lurline Gardens down the edge of the common. It appeared to have been a quiet night and there was no sign of any serious bomb damage – until they turned into their road and saw that their house and the one next door had taken a hit. The buildings were still standing, but the front wall had been blown open and the contents of the rooms had been reduced to steaming rubble. Fortunately, this time nobody was killed or injured. Nell and Ted walked stunned among the debris, picking up something here and there, but little of their furniture and belongings had survived intact except for in one corner of what was the main downstairs room. Neatly piled up, against what was once a wall, were 20 undisturbed red volumes of *Pictorial Knowledge*.

XIX

Tom, Ted and Nell

There were more changes to Nell's physical environment in the first few years of the war than there had been in the first 50 of her life. The community had been battered, bruised and dispersed, and was in a constant state of flux. It was difficult to keep track of who was where. Those who had been bombed took refuge with families and friends whilst new accommodation was sought and many never came back. Nell found it most disturbing that the buildings, even streets, she had taken for granted had disappeared overnight. She had got used to family and friends dying and disappearing by now, but the one constant had been the physical landscape: the houses, the pubs, the schools, the shops and the churches. Now they too had become vulnerable, and unsettling, morale-sapping empty spaces had appeared where they once stood. It rocked the spirit and made Nell realise that absolutely nothing was certain any more.

Bill and Dolly had taken her in at their home in Vardens Road to begin with, whilst Lurline Gardens was repaired. This was back up St John's Hill way, not far past Clapham Junction, but was too far away from the Battersea Park area she loved for her liking. She got to know her older brother and his wife best during this time and was grateful for their hospitality and kindness. Bill was an older man now and this disconcerted her, as she realised that she was not too far behind. She could see their father and grandfather in him as he aged and that too prompted feelings of mortality. Bill was a simple man with simple tastes and was content to allow Dolly to boss him around and run their lives. He liked a pint in the Plough and to put on the occasional bet with the street bookies. He liked to go for walks. He shared an allotment with a neighbour over in Earlsfield and he would visit there most days and in season bring home the vegetables he had managed to grow on his small strip of land. Tom would sometimes tease Bill about this allotment, saying that he must have a young girl hidden in the potting shed because he spent so much time over there. Tom also claimed that the allotment scheme was a sop from the rich man to the poor man. The land, he said, that belonged to everyone was snatched by the people who became the ruling classes and the landowners, and they, in an effort to stop an uprising, *allotted* back small strips of land to the common people. In later years, parish councils had protected those rights and kept the system going. Tom said it was a flaming insult and that you'd never catch him being grateful to anyone for the privilege of cultivating a few square feet of a field that belonged to the people anyway. Bill didn't give two hoots, as long as it got him out of the house and away from his wife for some of the day. What Dolly said he did without demur. Nell could see he was not a man that courted confrontation and understood now why he had left home so early on. He could not cope with the difficulties that were arising in his parents' marriage and had decided to get out. Despite Bill outwardly living the life of a classic henpecked music-hall cockney husband, Nell could see that he was happy with his life and at ease with the world. Of all her brothers, Bill had experienced the least eventful life but that was no bad thing.

She was relieved when, in 1942, the council found her a place of her own at the top of the hill on Eland Road, just off Lavender Hill again. She was used to having her own house and she needed somewhere to re-form the family unit. Her boys also needed somewhere to come home to, as did Charlie Boy. From here, she could step out of her house and look down on the streets and yards where she was born and had lived for most of her life, then on to the horizon of the recently built Battersea Power Station. She liked that. The power station had fast become Battersea's most recognisable landmark. If you mentioned to outsiders that you hailed from Battersea nowadays, they knew the power station, the Dogs Home and the park in that order.

The first thing she did once ensconced in her new home was to fetch Charlie Boy, who had been living and recovering in a sanatorium down on the south coast. Considering the injuries he had sustained, his recovery had been remarkable. Although the skin grafts on his face and hands were plentiful, the surgeons had done a good job and his basic facial characteristics had been preserved. Nell could still see Maggs and his father in him. That the tip of his nose had been replaced was obvious, and his left eye drooped a little, being pulled down by tighter replacement skin. His ears were yet to be rebuilt where they had burnt away. The fashion for longer hair in 20 years' time would alleviate that particular problem. But despite these ravages, he was not unpleasant or shocking to look at. More of a handicap for him was that the injuries and trauma had left him with a pronounced twitch and a stutter. The doctors told him these would recede in time.

Nell took Charlie home, fed him up and got him into Raywood

Street School, the same one his pre-war pals attended. He had lost two years in hospital and she was determined to ensure he caught up with his education. In the evenings, they sat together and worked through *Pictorial Knowledge*. For Charlie, this was preferable to playing outside and having the other boys take the rise out of him over his twitch or his stutter. Despite knowing just how he had received his injuries, the teasing was relentless at school. Charlie Boy kept all this to himself, knowing that to tell his aunt Nell would just make matters ten times worse. He had once made the mistake of telling her about a teacher who had disciplined him for speaking in class when he hadn't. This teacher, a Mr Wilkins, had rapped Charlie across the knuckles with a ruler as punishment and he had come home quite upset.

'Were you talking in class, Charlie Boy?'

'No, I never said a word, Auntie Nell.'

That was enough for Nell and she said no more. She knew Charlie avoided talking completely, let alone in class, such was his embarrassment about his speech defect. The following day, as the boy sat in class, he was horrified to look up as the door swung open and see the large frame of his aunt looming in front of the class. She was dressed in her double-breasted heavy black overcoat with buttons the size of milk saucers and a hat with a large feather in it, and was brandishing an umbrella. Charlie felt physically sick with foreboding.

'You Mr Wilkins?' she demanded accusingly.

'I am that man,' responded the teacher, rising to his feet and smiling. 'And you are?'

'Well, I am that lady Mrs Knight. I'm Charlie Melchior's guardian. You 'it 'im with a ruler yesterday for something 'e didn't do.'

'Really, Mrs Knight, I think that is between me and the boy. Would you like to talk about this in the corridor?'

'No, I bleedin' wouldn't. We'll talk about it in 'ere. 'E wasn't talking in class. Case you ain't noticed, he don't like speaking too much. So if I 'ear about you striking him again, I'll be down 'ere and I'll wrap this round your bloody 'ead.'

She brandished the brolly under the teacher's chin as he sat back down in his chair, again signalling he did not want confrontation. Boys placed their hands over their mouths to suppress their laughter whilst Charlie burnt red, examining his scuffed shoes.

* * *

Tom died in 1944. He was 58 years of age. The first Nell knew of him being ill was when a woman turned up at Eland Road alleging that she was Tom's girlfriend.

'Girlfriend?' Nell recounted incredulously later. 'Called 'erself 'is girlfriend. Well, she were 65, if she were a day. Looked like she'd been round the block a few times too.'

Although Tom visited Nell regularly and often drank around Battersea, he remained quite secretive and Nell rarely knew where he was staying. His lady friend was called Martha and apparently Tom had been living with her in a flat in Earlsfield for the last ten years. It later emerged that she sometimes accompanied him on his jaunts around the country's racecourses. Martha told Nell that Tom was in hospital in Wimbledon and that he had been diagnosed with lung cancer.

'You'll 'ave to pack up the fags now, Tom,' admonished Nell when she plumped herself down next to his bed in the hospital and dropped her large leather handbag on his legs, causing the patient to wince.

'A bit too late now, Nell,' Tom countered calmly. 'They tell me I'm on the way out. They say they can give me some of this radiation treatment business, but all it will do is give me a couple more months.'

'That's nice of 'em, innit? You think they'd give a man some 'ope.'

'It's not their fault, I've got the cancer in me lungs and they say it will spread all over me body quite quickly. I'll be a gonner in a few weeks.'

'Oh, Tom,' moaned Nell, visibly deflating and unable to keep up the jocularity.

'Don't you go upsetting yerself, gel. Everything is in order. I ain't got no debts. There's a little bit put by to pay for me funeral and maybe a bit on top for you, Nell. I ain't got no kids to worry about or them me, and Martha, she'll be all right. She's as strong as an 'orse, that one. Looks like one too.' Tom allowed himself a chuckle at his own wit.

'Oh, but Tom, we'll all miss you. I'll miss you. That leaves just me and Bill.'

'Maybe Teddy?' ventured Tom, but then thought better of it. 'But look, Nell, we've all got to go. It's my turn. I ain't complaining. I'm nearly 60 years of age – a man can't ask for more than that. I've 'ad a good life. Enjoyed every minute. I got no regrets. Ain't upset too many people on the way through. I'd do the same again, I would. Don't get upset on my account. I'm 'appy. I ain't complaining.'

Tom wasn't complaining. He wasn't kidding either. The revelation of his imminent death had not fazed, upset or panicked him in any way; it was one of those things. Tom took everything in his stride, even his own death.

He surprised the doctors, though, and himself, by rallying and living for several months with the disease and then returning home to die. For a couple of weeks in the period when he revived, Nell thought that the brother she idolised was going to recover and bounce back like he always did. That would be typical of Tom. But then he plummeted, and Nell cursed the Lord and how He would sometimes raise hopes when people were dying. He really shouldn't throw out that rope of optimism to which loved ones cling. It was cruel and there was no need for it. Nell visited often when he was back home in bed and warmed to Martha, who she admired for the way she nursed her brother as he wasted away in front of their eyes. Nell could not help but see the irony of one of the final, lasting memories she had of Tom. He was lying on top of the bed in his pyjamas, his tanned, leathery skin hanging from the now prominent bones on his arms and legs. Martha was sitting on the edge of the bed supporting Tom's head and tenderly holding a Senior Service to his lips whilst he inhaled and then slowly removing it again until he mustered the strength for the next draw. According to Martha, he smoked two cigarettes on the day he died.

In later decades, when medical experts proved the link between smoking and lung disease, Nell felt vindicated. She told people she had been saying this for years – and she probably had. However, it did not explain why she continued to smoke into her ninth decade. The rules, even when she set them, did not apply to her. Another one of her sweeping statements was that, until the Second World War, it was mainly men who smoked, and it was the stress and fear of the bombing that drove the womenfolk of Britain to embrace cigarettes. Again, anecdotal evidence has Nell and her mother smoking regularly even before the First World War.

Back down at Streatham Vale cemetery for Tom's funeral, Nell noticed that a large memorial had been erected. After her brother was put into the ground, she wandered over to look at it. It was a curved, white stone decorated with the names of those local men who had given their lives in the 1914–18 war. As her eyes passed down the names, she started when she got to Sapper Henry Knight. She stopped in silent reflection for a few minutes, shocked that her late husband had suddenly been remembered, nearly a quarter of a century on, somewhere else outside of the family. During those few minutes, though, as she stood studying the memorial, the initial pleasure and pride in her find turned into a simmering anger.

'Marvellous, ain't it?' she spat to her brother, Bill. 'The only way people like us get an 'eadstone and a decent burial is to "give" our lives in a war and then we 'ave to share it with 200 of the other poor bastards. And 'oo says my poor 'Enry *gave* his bleedin' life? 'E never *gave* his life. None of 'em did. *They* took it. Other people took it. It should say "whose lives was tooken". What d'ya reckon, Bill?'

'I reckon you're right, Nell. Still, you should be proud 'e's got a stone. 'E's the first in our family and that's saying something. 'Arry and Ted will be pleased, I'm sure.'

'They'd rather 'ave their father around than a bloody stone. I'd rather 'ave a husband around than a stone.'

'I know, Nell. You're right.'

Bill slipped his arm around his sister's waist, flattened down his cap and guided Nell towards the big gates. Brother and sister: the last surviving children of Edward and Annie Bradshaw.

XX

A New Husband

The war ended and the British were victorious again, although Nell didn't feel very victorious. There was no celebrating in the street for her. No flocking to Trafalgar Square or chest swelling with national pride. The war was a bastard. She never understood how, later on, people could look back on it with such a warm nostalgia, Britain's finest hour and all that. This new war killed millions again and wrecked the lives of those that survived.

To Nell, it seemed a lifetime since the German bombers had slaughtered Maggs and the children. She had lost her sister and her nieces, her house of twenty years, and her network of friends, relatives and colleagues in those six long years. Everyone's life had been permanently truncated. Now there was an age that was 'before the war' and one that was 'after the war'. Nell preferred the former. She belonged to the world before the war and was a stranger in this new age, however much the people that were at ease with it tried to make her welcome. Countless friends and relatives were now scattered around south London and beyond. Thankfully, both her boys returned home in good shape and, for a short time at least, they all lived in Eland Road together. Nell was relieved and happy to have her family partially re-formed and to be looking after her boys again.

Battersea had changed for ever. Not only had the war displaced families that had shared the same streets for generations but also a continual process of slum clearance before, during and after the war had had a similar effect. Many cynically joked that the Germans merely did the town planners' jobs for them. Streets were bulldozed with little thought for the communities that were supposed to be thankful for the offer of a 'modern' flat, even if it did mean the dispersal of their neighbourhood. Swapping a way of life for the privilege of a 'bathroom with all the mod cons' never seemed much of a deal to Nell. In the 1920s and '30s, Nell could walk down Battersea Park Road and know two out of every three people she passed. By 1950, two out of three people in the street were strangers to her. She estimated that of the people that lived around her in 1935 only a quarter were still in those same houses 20 years later. The upheaval, the new circumstances and alterations to the physical environment were difficult for Nell to come to terms with, but she gathered her defences and fought a one-woman crusade against change for the rest of her life, although even she could see that the post-war world did have an upside. The flats that were being built on the sites of Wadhurst Road and the like did offer the luxury of electricity, a bathroom and privacy. She could see why the younger generation could not believe their luck, but they were not for her and she was most offended to keep hearing of her old homes being referred to coldly as slums.

Maybe it was this sense of dislocation and general post-war melancholy that caused Nell to take a step she would never have considered seriously in earlier days. It was out of character and it came out of the blue, surprising both her family and herself. It was a story Nell often told in a simplistic, dismissive fashion but the bones of which were undoubtedly correct.

There was a butcher's shop on Battersea Park Road that Nell used even after she left neighbouring Lurline Gardens. The owners knew the family well, especially Nell and her mother. Her boys can remember her bowling into the shop demanding the best cuts of meat and almost without fail complaining about the previous purchase being 'too chewy' or 'stringy'. The old butcher never argued, always making happy and cheerful conversation, even though Nell would then cut him dead mid-flow by asking haughtily, 'I 'ope you've washed your 'ands before 'andling my meat.'

One day, she ran into Jim Tregent in the shop. The Tregents had lived close to the Bradshaws for years, and Jim and his father, both being printers on the newspaper, enjoyed a more regular and higher level of income than many of the local men.

'Nell Bradshaw! Well, I never. 'Ow are you keeping? Where you gorn to?'

'Mrs Knight to you, Jim Tregent. I'm over Eland Road with my two boys. You still down Corunna with the old man?'

'Lord, no. 'E snuffed it, Nell. Didn't you 'ear? A while back, that was. No, I'm living with my sister and her 'usband just down the road. I'm retired now, Nell. Packed up. No more nights and no more traipsing up to Fleet Street. I've got a bit of money in the bank and old Lord Rothermere pays me a fair pension, so I ain't complaining. But it's a crime, Nell, I've got a comfortable life and no one to share it with. Ain't you thought about getting spliced again, Nell? Can't be much fun being a widder and gettin' old on yer own.'

'No, I ain't. I've got me family. Anyway, you've been on yer own all yer life, why you start bellyaching now?'

'Working nights don't make it easy, Nell, do it? It were 'ard to court a young lady when I was in me bed asleep all day. Anyway, all I want is some company in me old age. I don't ask for any more. We've always got on well and I reckon you could do with some company too, Nell. So if you want to get married, Nell, just say the word.'

'Jim Tregent, are you asking me to marry you?'

'That's right.'

''Ow dare you! Bleedin' cheek. In the butcher's shop! Who do you think I am? Who do you think you are? You must be senile, you must. You silly old git. Be off with you, Jim Tregent.'

Despite her incredulity and the perceived temerity of Jim Tregent's offer in the butcher's shop, Nell gave consideration to the proposal. Her boys had already broken their permanent ties with the family home – the war had seen to that – and she felt young Charlie would leave as soon as he physically could; her parents and husband were long dead and only one of her siblings survived. Nell was beginning to feel lonely and she knew she could only get lonelier. Money was not as tight as it used to be, but she still had to graft and she wasn't getting any younger. It would be nice not to *have* to crawl around on all-fours scrubbing other people's floors. If Jim Tregent would agree to some ground rules, she could see some merit in his offer. She didn't love him and she couldn't possibly believe that he loved her, but they did always get on. They shared a history. They knew all the same people and places and had been through similar trials and tribulations. She wrestled with a few things – What would her boys say? Was she betraying Henry? What would her mother think if she were alive? Was it fair on Jim Tregent himself? Was she marrying a man for his little bit of money? – but she soon rationalised those. The boys and Charlie might not jump up and down with joy at the prospect of a new man in the house, but they would not begrudge it. She knew deep inside her that Henry really did wish her to have a happy life, and if this made her happier and things easier he would approve; but she did expect to go to her grave without having formed a relationship with another man, whatever her former husband thought. Her mother might not have been overjoyed, but she was not here. And as far as the money question went, well, Jim Tregent himself had laid out his stall: a small lift in her standard of living underpinned his offer.

A fortnight after accusing Jim Tregent of being senile, she met him again in the street. 'Jim, I've been thinking 'bout what you said the uvver week. I've been thinking it might not be a bad idea. You could move in with me. I could look after you and maybe I could cut down on me little cleaning jobs.'

'That's marvellous, Nell, bloody marvellous. And what about getting wed?'

'Well, of course we'd get wed, you daft ha'p'orth. I ain't gonna live in sin, am I? But Jim, I 'ave to tell you I'm not for sex.'

'Lord Almighty, Nell, don't chew worry abaht that. I'm an old man. I'm not for all that stuff. Stand on me. No, no, I jus' want to grow old with you. 'Ave cups of tea, listen to the radio, go to the pictures and down the seaside. You're a fine woman and always 'ave been, Nell.'

Jim's words struck a chord. He was a thoroughly decent man. She had to stop herself putting down her wicker shopping basket, standing on tiptoe and kissing him.

Nell and Jim married with the minimum of fuss at the register office. There was no party and the only guests were Jim's sister and Nell's brother, Bill, who acted as witnesses. A few drinks were shared in the Young's pub in Wandsworth before walking up the hill and home.

They quickly adapted to the life of a long-married couple with incredible ease. Jim had very simple tastes. He smoked his Gold

Flake tobacco and passed many hours carefully rolling his cigarettes, starting to smoke them, then nipping them for return to his tobacco tin and a final smoke later. He hungrily read his newspapers. He took the *News Chronicle* and *Evening News* daily and the *Express* and the *News of the World* on a Sunday. He enjoyed his radio shows and walks in the park. He did not really drink. He did not go to the pub as a matter of course but would take alcohol at Christmas and other celebrations. A lifetime of working nights had conditioned him to sleep in the day and he was prone to take two or three naps before bedtime. Nell carried on as before, although she did cut right back on her cleaning, keeping just a couple of light local jobs. She could afford to buy a nice joint every Sunday now and kept some Guinness in the house. They went to the pictures every week and during the summer travelled on the train down to Hastings, Brighton and Margate, where they happily spent the day sitting on the beach on adjacent deckchairs looking out over the Channel, exchanging few words. Life with dollops of leisure time thrown in and some green notes as well as coins in her purse was very agreeable. The only downside, as far as Nell was concerned, was that Jim's arrival almost certainly accelerated the flight of her boys from the nest. But they were going to fly anyway and she happily swapped the few months, or maybe a year, she lost of their company for her new lifestyle.

Harry landed a job with the Water Board and thus became the first Battersea Knight or Bradshaw to work in an office. Nell saw this as a great achievement and would tell anyone that asked that her boy was a 'clerical'. Enquirers were left wondering if her eldest son had perhaps joined the Church. None of the family probably appreciated it at the time but Harry had also taken the family link with the River Thames into another generation. Ted, meanwhile, had returned home from the war and tried to trace his old mucker Harry Cousins with an eye to resuming where they had left off.

But Harry had shrewdly set up business importing Italian foods into England and he had based himself mainly in Rome. Reluctantly, Ted took work as a labourer, biding his time by keeping busy with the urgent rebuilding schedule that was already under way, whilst waiting for an opportunity.

Charlie was never able to catch up on the schooling he had missed, and when he left school at 15 years of age he had no real idea what work he would or could go into. He lacked the basic education to go 'clerical' but was not suited to heavy manual work either. Between them, he and Nell decided to look around for an apprenticeship of some sort. He had a gift for constructing Meccano models and Nell believed this stood him in some stead to be accepted as an apprentice engineer somewhere. Charlie was less confident and worried about operating in the big world altogether, although he would never have let on to his aunt that he was unhappy, unsettled and nervous. He was forever grateful to Aunt Nell for taking him in, but he had effectively been orphaned and dealing with bereavement, trauma, physical disability and displacement all at the same time levied a terrible strain. Nevertheless, Nell got him in at Dorman Long, a large engineering and bridge-building company down the road, and Charlie buckled down to an apprenticeship.

In 1948, at the age of 60, Nell took her first-ever holiday, barring the Lady Ware-sponsored trip to Ireland, when she and Jim took themselves off for a week's stay in a guest house on the front at St Leonards – a mile's walk down Bottle Alley from the familiar day-trip territory of Hastings. They had a glorious time, visiting the theatre, watching the shows on the pier and sampling the pubs and fish-and-chip shops of Hastings' old town. Nell even dragged poor old Jim up the East Hill and attempted to retrace the walk she and Henry had done 30 years earlier when he had returned home emaciated from the First World War. A lifetime of cleaning, scrubbing and walking to and from her jobs had kept Nell fit and healthy, but Jim had lived a more sedentary lifestyle in the compositors' room of the newspaper. He had taken buses and trams to and from work and this, coupled with a voracious smoking habit, had rendered him a fairly frail, out-of-condition 64-year-old man.

'Come on, Jim, we need to get to Fairlight before Christmas,' goaded Nell, as her husband paused with his hands on his hips and surveyed the climb up Ecclesbourne Glen.

Resignedly, Jim followed her up the steep, winding steps, fighting for breath and wondering how, even if they turned back now, he would get home without his lungs collapsing completely. Oblivious to this, Nell stopped to look at a house perched precariously on the cliff edge, whose garden had fallen ominously into the sea.

'Bloody 'ell, look at that. Fancy waking up and finding your front garden gorn. Wouldn't catch me living on a bleedin' cliff. You'd never sleep at night.'

There was no reply from Jim. Nell looked around to see her husband writhing on the grass, gasping for breath, like a goldfish tipped out of his bowl. She thought he would die there and then, and she sat down and placed his head in her lap and stroked his head. Slowly, he regained his composure and eventually they struck inland to find less hilly land and head back to Hastings.

'Soon as we get 'ome you're seeing a doctor, Jim Tregent. That ain't right. Clapsing like that after walking up a tiny 'ill.'

Jim didn't want to go to the doctor. As far as he was concerned, dragging a 64-year-old man up and down cliffs was bound to result in some disastrous consequences. Just because Nell could do it didn't mean he could. It was foolhardy and he would never have undertaken it had he known the task ahead. His wife was insane – she'd probably attempt Everest if challenged. The other reason he didn't want to go to the doctor was that, in his experience, it always ended in tears. His uncle had gone in with pains in his leg and had come out of hospital a few weeks later with the leg having gone. His father had complained to his doctor of a pain in his mouth and, next thing he knew, he was in hospital too and died within weeks apparently of cancer of the soft palate. No, Jim was distrustful of doctors and hospitals, and although he set out one morning to satisfy Nell and see his doctor, he deceived her and spent the morning listening to the band on Clapham Common.

'What did 'e say?' quizzed Nell on his return.

'Doctor says I'm fine. 'E says my lungs are as strong as bellows and the 'eart is ticking well. 'E says I shouldn't go walking up bloody great mountains at my age, that's all.'

'What'd 'e say about your roll-ups?' Nell had a theory that smoking roll-ups was damaging his lungs or heart, or both – paradoxically, the Weights non-tipped that she smoked were almost health-giving.

''E said they were fine,' lied Jim.

Six months after the fabled hillwalk, Jim was sitting in his armchair having just finished dinner whilst Nell washed the dishes in the kitchen. She heard him groan, so came out of the kitchen, wiping her hands on her apron. Jim was leaning forward clutching his chest and as she eased him backwards, she could see he was in serious trouble. She ran across the street to ask a family who she knew had a telephone to call an ambulance. When she went back inside, Jim was dead. He had lurched forward onto the floor, having suffered a second heart attack.

When the doctor came, she berated him for not having diagnosed Jim's failing heart.

'I can assure you, Mrs Tregent, I have not seen your husband for any ailment whatsoever in years,' he replied.

Shame on you, she thought. The lengths to which professional people went to shirk their responsibility incensed her but now was not the time to have a row. Less than a week later, she buried Jim. They had not been married even three years.

XXI

The Swinging '60s

In 1951, Nell finally became the last surviving child of Edward and Annie Bradshaw. Brother Bill died in his sleep at the age of 73. Nell had thought it was the best way for him to go (and she hoped her passing would be much the same) until she spoke to Dolly, who explained that on the night of his death Bill had been tossing, turning and groaning in bed and that she could remember him murmuring, 'Help me, Dolly. Help me.' But she had dismissed it as him talking in his sleep, as apparently he often did, and told him to belt up. She even gave him a kick for good measure. When she awoke in the morning, Bill was lying there next to her, mouth open, lips blue and stone-cold dead.

By the time Bill died and the family, what was left of it, assembled yet again at Streatham Vale cemetery, Nell was the only mourner among them born before the turn of the century. She was living alone in Battersea, as she would for the rest of her days. Her boys had long flown the nest. Harry had been moved to the

Sutton Water Company and had met his future wife, Eileen, who worked in the typing pool. They married the following year and as Harry's career progressed up the clerical and then management ladder, their homes grew in line with the size of their family and his improving wage packet; the word 'promotion' entered Nell's vocabulary – ''Arry was up for promotion, you know.'

He and Eileen finally settled with five children in a spacious semi-detached house in leafy Cheam. Nell noticed that as Harry entered his 30s and then his 40s, his accent and speech altered in line with his changing affluence. At some point, he must have made the decision to bend down and scoop up his aitches. Nell did not mind, did not feel he had betrayed his roots in any way: his great-grandfather had done the very same thing 100 years before to make his way in life.

A year after his brother, Ted married a Clapham Common flower-shop girl called Anne and they would eventually have four children. It took Ted a few years to find his vocation but find it he did. Gino, the man who ran the coffee stall next to the gates of Battersea Park and who had spent so much time with poor old Sam propping up his bar, won the Irish lottery and bought himself a café under Dogs Home bridge and gave all of his children a few hundred pounds each. His son, Luca, was friendly with Ted and they decided to set up a business selling and laying Italian marble floors to the wealthy and used Luca's few hundred pounds to get the business off the ground. It started slowly, but as Britain became more prosperous, and more and more houses were built, L&E Marble grew bigger and bigger. Ted's greatest regret was that he was unable to provide any capital at the time the company was formed and although his contribution to the business in all other ways was equal to that of Luca's, for the next 50 years he was entitled to 35 per cent of the profits compared to his partner's 65 per cent. Despite this, Ted became comfortable and by the 1970s was living in a large detached house in Haywards Heath.

Nell's pride in her boys was immeasurable. It was hard for her to digest how well they had actually got on in life. The notion of having your own stairs, carpets, bathrooms, televisions, cars, washing machines, telephones and, in the early days, electricity was all very hard to assimilate. Although they took her down to their houses as much as she would allow, she was not relaxed in the green idyll of Surrey or Sussex. The excessive space in the rooms and the dull throb of technology all around unsettled her, and she was forever agitating inside to be taken back to Battersea and her small, dark, cluttered rooms in Eland Road. It was the brave new world she had heard about, which had been much heralded, but she was too old to enter it. Her boys had achieved a luxurious life and that was excellent, but she had no wish to join them in it.

She was even more proud of young Charlie Melchior. At the tender age of 16, he had left Nell and moved to Crawley in Surrey, where he had embarked on a new life. He chose Crawley because it was a new town. A new town with new people, he figured. There was no past and he could start afresh among others who were starting anew. He had received some form of compensation for his injuries and first he tried to give this to Nell in return for her having cared for him. She would have none of it and told him to use it in whichever way he could. Despite his young age, Charlie Boy chucked in at Dorman's, having made his mind up to make this new life on his own. He apprenticed himself to a car mechanic and learnt this relatively new and burgeoning trade whilst living in cheap digs. Charlie was keen to work long hours and soon became an expert mechanic. Customers often insisted that Charlie looked after their vehicles, such was his dedication and growing reputation. His colleagues joked that Charlie was only happy when lying down under a car and that his feet were far more recognisable to all than his face. The garage owner, Mr

Bradbury, admitted that having Charlie was equal to employing three mechanics and when he was only in his early 20s, he was made a partner. Around the same time, he moved in with the Bradburys as a lodger.

As car ownership increased, business boomed. New premises were acquired on the outskirts of town but still on the main road and they started to sell petrol from the pump. Charlie grew in confidence as each year went by and began courting June, Mr Bradbury's daughter, and they were married in 1957. When Mr Bradbury succumbed to cancer in 1962, he surprised everyone by leaving the business to Charlie on the condition he looked after his widow, which he did assiduously until her death some 25 years later.

Every other Sunday, Charlie drove up to Battersea for dinner with Nell. It was a ritual they both enjoyed. Nell referred to those two days of the month as 'Charlie Sunday'; she couldn't do this or that on that day because it was a Charlie Sunday.

When Charlie Boy and June married, they held their reception at the posh Burford Bridge Hotel, nestling at the foot of the Surrey beauty spot Box Hill. Charlie made a speech that had Harry and Ted and their wives filling up with tears and Nell puffing up with pride and dabbing her eyes with a handkerchief. His difficulty in controlling his stutter at emotional times such as this made the tribute all the more moving. He said, 'I'd also like to thank and salute the lady sitting opposite – my auntie Nell, my mum's older sister. In our family, Nell was the one everyone looked up to and everyone turned to when they were in trouble. My mother idolised her and after my father died she looked after me and my dear sisters so my mother could go out to work and earn a living. And it wasn't as if she didn't have enough on her own plate. Her husband had died in the first war and she struggled to raise my two cousins, Harry and Ted, and what a good job she did. Not all of you will know this, but when we were blitzed in London in 1940, my house took a direct hit and Mum and my sisters, Violet, Mary and Nell, all perished. I was the only one to survive. I was badly injured and burnt, and spent many months in a succession of hospitals, but wherever I was, Nell came to see me every week. She was all I had and when I was well enough to come out, she took me in and loved me. She gave me a home and helped me heal, got me back into school and encouraged me to start my life again. I thank you for that, Aunt Nell, from the bottom of my heart. I'd like to raise a glass to Aunt Nell and to all those who can't be here today, especially my mum and dad, and dear Violet, Mary and Nell, whose lives were cut so tragically short. To Nell Tregent, the finest woman to come out of Battersea.'

By this time, Charlie's speech had drowned in its own tears. His new wife stood up and cradled his head into her breast and eased him back into his seat, as the response to the toast was lost in tearful applause.

In the early 1960s, the council moved Nell across the road into a purpose-built flat on Mysore Road. Eland Road had been comfortable, especially after the gas was turned off and electricity routed in, but Mysore Road was of a luxury she could not have anticipated only a few years earlier. There was a separate bathroom with a novel ceramic peach-coloured bath that she never sat in once, instead using it as a large tub for washing clothes, and a small kitchen with an electric oven, hot water on tap and a large lounge that was big enough to contain her bed. She had lived in similar floor spaces before, but as she was now the only person occupying these rooms they seemed to her to be positively enormous.

Harry brought her a television set, which at first she treated as an unwelcome guest and would only use sparingly. She could not believe that by switching it on she was not burdening the country's energy resources or, worse still, racking up her own electricity bill to a tremendous level. She also took some years to get over the urge to knock up any neighbours she thought might not have a TV and share this luxury with them. Over time, though, she accepted it and it became her chief companion. After a few years, she had acquainted herself with the likes of Bruce Forsyth, Harry Worth, Morecambe and Wise, Tommy Trinder and Tommy Cooper. But the television still did unsettle her at times. She could never quite get to grips with how it worked and that the people appearing on the screen were not actually addressing her personally. Her habit of replying to them was amusing to start with but later infuriated her grandchildren when she came to stay at Christmas. In her final years, as her grip on reality ebbed and flowed, she made tea for two: one for her, and one for whoever was on the television.

She found it hard not to become personally embroiled in the news that flickered away on her screen. She used to read the newspaper at her own pace, filtering what she decided to take in or not; now this box in her room was firing out such vivid messages and information it unnerved her. In 1966, when a man called Harry Roberts shot and killed three policemen in west London then went on the run, she became convinced that he was hiding out in the flat above her.

'How do you know he is?' asked the weary desk sergeant at Lavender Hill police station, which was unluckily for them just across the road from Nell's flat.

'Because I've bloody well seen him lurking round the stairwell, ain't I? I see 'im and 'e runs straight up the stairs. There's only one door up there. 'Ers. Missus Fulford's. She's taken 'im in, Gawd knows why. She's simple. You best get over there before 'e kills 'er an all.'

It was a tough one for the policeman. He was 99.9 per cent sure that the old lady was barking mad, but if they didn't investigate and Harry Roberts had been hiding out across the road from their very own police station, there would be hell to pay. On the other hand, if they were to visit the flat to check out a police-murderer's presence, a fully armed operation would have to be mounted. Sensibly, a couple of officers were assigned to watch the flat until they were convinced that Mrs Fulford was, as they suspected, a little old lady living entirely alone. Meanwhile, the desk sergeant rang her son Harry to explain the situation and hint that his mother may need some care.

Harry was infuriated to find, on his arrival to rebuke his mother, Nell standing outside her front door, shopping bags around her feet, engaged in friendly conversation with the very lady who she had just told the police was harbouring Britain's most-wanted criminal.

Ted had an equally bizarre experience when he visited her once. As she let him in the door, he followed her into the main room, where she pointed out the television, which was off. 'Take that bloody thing away,' she demanded.

'Why, Mum? What's up?'

'That Max Miller came on. I don't want 'im anywhere near me.'

'Just get up and switch it off, Mum, or turn over to the other side. You know how to do that. What's wrong with Max Miller anyway?'

'Did you seem 'im the other night, on the P'ladium? Did you see 'im?'

Ted presumed that his mother was objecting to some near-the-knuckle joke from the popular comedian. 'Yes, Mum, I saw him. He was very funny, I thought.'

She beckoned her son towards her and whispered, ''E's Tichy, that's who he is. Tichy bleedin' Thorogood.'

'Give over, Mum. Tichy swung 30 years ago or more. What are you talking about?'

''E looks like 'im, 'e talks like 'im and 'e dresses like 'im. It must be 'is son. And I don't need to be looking at the likes of 'im.'

'His name is Miller. He comes from Brighton. He's nothing to do with Tichy Thorogood.'

'You look it up somewhere, boy. Miller problee ain't his real name. 'E's problee changed it. And if it is 'is real name, 'e's problee his bastard son. There was enough of them, I'll tell you.'

There was no persuading Nell and the thoroughly innocent Max Miller was added to the list of names not to be mentioned around the old lady. This put the cheeky chappie in the doubtful company of Tichy himself, Adolf Hitler, Lord Haw Haw and the ironmonger on Lavender Hill, who she believed was a secret sex maniac with unnatural designs on her flesh. Ted went home that afternoon and told his wife that he thought Nell was losing it and perhaps they should take her television away.

The boys also attempted to introduce a telephone into Nell's flat but on this point she was adamant. She had never had a telephone and had managed perfectly well, she said, so why on earth should she need one at this point in her life? Harry and Ted pointed out that she was growing older and that she could fall or become ill and that if she did they would not be able to get to her quickly. This did not wash.

'Besides,' she told them, 'I don't want to be talking to strangers all day long.' It was impossible to convince her that a phone was not a gadget whereby people unknown to one another could make contact, like CB radio or the Internet many years later.

The television was confusing enough and she seemed to believe that telephones allowed outsiders to look into her little flat at will. She was having none of that malarkey.

When she reached the age of 80, she made the decision that she ought to give up work. By this stage, she was cleaning only for Mrs Lowther, now the widow of Dr Lowther, and she was finding the bus journey and bending over more and more of a chore.

'I've decided to retire, madam. I 'ope you don't mind. I'm finding the work 'arder. I'll stay on until you can find someone else, if you like.'

'Mrs Tregent, of course you should retire if you're finding things difficult. Oh, my goodness, of course you should. Do you mind me asking, Mrs Tregent, how old you are?'

'Yes, madam. I was seventy-nine last week.'

At this point, Mrs Lowther fainted (at least she did in Nell's telling of the story).

Harry and Ted organised a surprise 80th party down at Cheam for Nell. Ted drove up to collect her and Nell thought she was being brought down merely for Sunday lunch. When she was shown into the front room, to a sea of what should have been familiar faces holding glasses aloft, hip-hip-hooraying, her reaction was typical. 'What you lot doing 'ere?'

This raised a laugh from all of those who thought she was joking. She cussed her son for allowing her to come to a party unprepared. She'd have brought her favourite handbag, which her sons teased her was bigger and heavier than Dr Finlay's medical bag, she'd have got the butterfly brooch out and maybe had her hair done. She was not at all happy about the imposition and was not shy about letting this be known. Only an hour or so in, and after Harry had forced three sherries down her, did she relax and allow herself to enjoy the occasion. There were grandchildren and nephews and nieces galore, who had to remind Nell whose offspring they were each time they spoke to her or offered her another cheesy stick. But Harry and Ted had done well in finding a few older faces to add to the occasion. Mrs Lowther arrived and stayed a short while, causing Nell to revert to status and stand for the whole time she was present.

'She's a doctor's wife, not the Duchess of Argyll, Mum,' whispered Ted. Bill's Bill, now a pensioner himself, was there, looking more and more like his father, and this pleased Nell no end. Sam's eldest, Ernie, now in his 40s, brought her a framed photo of his father that she treasured ever after, and John Knight and his wife, son of her late husband's brother, who she had not seen for nearly 50 years since he was a lad, presented her with a picture he had painted of a lone lighterman rowing on the Thames in the shadow of Tower Bridge. This was the unexpected success of the evening and caused Nell to fill up with tears.

'Speech!' shouted someone as Nell regarded the painting, clutching it tightly.

'On yer bike!'

XXII

Stranded

As she entered her ninth decade, all three boys were keen to move Nell out of Battersea and nearer to one of them. Ted would have happily taken her into his house in Sussex, whilst Charlie and Harry recognised her need for independence and wanted her to take a flat close by. There was no longer an infrastructure around her and the community she knew had long since dispersed or died off. Even though Nell did not worry, her boys were concerned for her personal safety now. Things had changed. Cars filled up the Battersea roads now. Nell always saw them as impudent impostors on 'their' roads and always crossed streets, often laden with shopping, without any attempt to wait for a gap in the traffic. She was not a child and would not be looking left or right and practising the Green Cross Code. In earlier times, shocked motorists would apply their brakes and wait patiently for the lady to make it across to the other side of the road; now they sounded their horns and shouted abuse from their windows: 'Look where yer going, you silly old cow!'

Her boys feared it would only be a matter of time before drivers, no longer guests but owners of the highways, crashed straight into her. Crime was on the up, whatever the authorities claimed about it being only the fear of crime that was rising: after all, people aren't stupid – if things start happening to them and those around them that never used to, that tells them more than any statistics. Nell knew friends who had had their handbags snatched, she spoke to neighbours who had suffered break-ins and she could constantly hear the sirens outside her windows. 'You'd hear them once in a blue moon in the old days,' Nell often mused.

Unfairly but predictably Nell attributed the rise in crime entirely to the influx of immigrants into London. Harry was with her one summer's evening in the 1970s when she threw open her window and began shouting at a group of black children sitting smoking on the small wall outside the flats.

'Go on, clear orf! Get back to yer own country.'

Harry hurriedly shut the window and pulled his mother back from the curtains. As far as he could see, the children were doing no more than chatting and being kids. 'Mum, you've got to stop that. This *is* their country. They live here and were probably born here – they're not doing anything wrong. They're kids, for God's sake. You'll have problems if you start hollering and swearing at them.'

'But they're everywhere, boy. Flaming perishers, all of 'em. This road is full of 'em. They sauce you all the time and the parents don't care. They're not our people, 'Arry. Nobody asked us if we wanted them to come 'ere. Nobody asked anyone. They just put 'em 'ere. Don't we 'ave a say? This was our town and they just put 'em 'ere. They didn't put 'em in their towns, did they? 'Ow many did they put in Cadogan Square? 'Ow many live in the rich towns? They don't even want to be 'ere anyway. They don't like us people and they don't like England. It's too cold for 'em.'

Stranded

Harry could see his mother was upset and possibly a little bit scared. 'Mum, nobody asked them when we went into their countries years ago. We conquered their countries and made them part of the Commonwealth. They have a right to come, and people forget it but we asked them to.'

Nell grunted, which signified she did not agree but saw no point in pursuing the point further. Harry felt for her – it was not the Battersea *he* knew, loved and understood either, let alone the place that coursed through his mother's veins.

'Look, Mum, I know we've said it before, but why don't you come down to Cheam. If you're not happy here, you don't have to stay.'

Nell waved her forefinger in his direction like he was a teenager again and had tried on a bit of backchat. 'Course I'm 'appy. I've 'ad worse than a few nig nogs lipping me. I'm not leaving my flat. I'm not leaving Battersea. They'll 'ave to carry me out of 'ere. I belong 'ere. I just don't like the wogs sitting on my wall all day long. 'Itler never drove me out and neither will they.'

Harry stood wincing at every 'wog', 'nigger' and 'coon' that tumbled from his mother's lips. He knew she wasn't the sort of person who would limit this terminology to the privacy of her own home and the thought of it put the fear of God into him. He also knew how she would react if someone attempted to mug her and steal her pension. Her hardening in attitude to her West Indian neighbours saddened Harry for he could remember 20 years earlier, when the first wave of immigrants started arriving in London, and the family that had moved into the house across the road. It was winter and they'd see the father leaving the house for work in the morning in slacks and a thin cotton shirt.

'Look at 'im,' Nell said as she shook her head. ''E'll catch his death. You think the Guvverment would tell 'em that it might be 'ot in Jermaker but it ain't 'ot in London.'

A few days later, Harry passed the West Indian man in the street and he flashed a broad grin at him. Harry responded with a nod and a smile and had to look twice, as the new arrival was now dressed in an ill-fitting but sturdy pin-stripe suit over the same flimsy floral cotton shirt. It was only as he put his key into the door that he remembered from where he recognised the garb: it was his very own demob suit, which had been hanging in the wardrobe since 1945.

Only in the final decade of her life did her attitude to black people noticeably soften. This was when she slowly but surely became extremely fond of her district nurse, Mrs Bruno. (Or Mrs Bronco, as she annoyingly called her. In these later years, she called people by names that somehow fitted her mental image of them and she did not care what anyone thought. Mrs Bruno became Bronco because she was big and strong. One can only speculate why singer Shirley Bassey was always referred to as Shirley Brassey.) She saw through colour for the first time and found a kind woman who had raised a good family against the odds. Her own son had been a handful for a time but was now establishing himself as a promising boxer.

During her 80s and 90s, Nell settled into a routine of contented retirement. The Stanley Arms had changed its name now to the Cornet and Horse and every weekday lunchtime Nell visited for a Guinness and a ham sandwich. The place was full of memories for her but contained nobody to share them with. This was where Tichy Thorogood had caught his sister's eye in the big whisky mirror and mouthed 'I love you' a lifetime and more ago. She and her mother and Henry had spent countless other quieter evenings in the pub. The memories and the ghosts were enough to make Nell feel at home there and the modern clientele regarded her in the same light as the framed picture postcards of Battersea past that hung on the walls around the bar – an interesting and sometimes entertaining window on local history. Except Nell lived and spoke. The 'clericals' from the council offices nearby became accustomed to her joining their conversations uninvited, as they filled their lunch breaks with a lager and a ploughman's.

'Don't talk to me about prices. Everyfing's so dear now. 'Ow they think we can live on a pension when you need a king's ransom just to buy a loaf and some milk, I don't know. 'Ow you young men keep your families, I don't know. Of course, they're giving all our money to the Common Market. You know that, don't you? And what do we get from them? Bugger all. When did you 'ear your shopkeeper say, "Don't worry, love, your groceries are a pound cheaper today because the French have just put a load of money into the Common Market?" Course you don't! I never asked to join the Common Market, did you? Course not. Nobody asked us. It was that useless lump Edwood 'Eath. It was all right for 'im. He lives in Broadstairs. It don't affect him.'

Nobody had talked to Nell about prices.

The rest of her day was punctuated with a bit of shopping and visits to Lavender Hill police station to complain about the ever increasing cost of the aforesaid shopping or the size of her electricity and gas bills. She came from an age when the police came from the community and helped the community. Despite her boys' protestations, she visited regularly and the ever changing desk sergeants treated her eccentricity with tact and understanding. She had seen decimalisation in 1971 as a sinister development from Europe (engineered by the Germans) and refused to understand money thereafter. 'What's that in real money?' she demanded gruffly of exasperated shopkeepers well into the 1980s before fishing into her purse and paying for anything.

The fact that she belonged to another world was always in evidence and it became amplified the older she became and the more her peers dropped from view. Her greeting of 'Plenty of work?' rather than 'How are you?' seemed more curious as the years went by, and as mass unemployment and economic depression became a more distant memory.

Her urgings to her grandchildren to always finish what was on their plate was grounded in her experience of true hunger and food deprivation. Her sons found her constant forebodings unsettling and they attempted to shield their children from her proclamations on the imminent demise of the world. They didn't want to be told that they must not trust the Germans, or the Russians come to that, and to be forever asked whether they were conserving food and preparing for unemployment, war or worse. They liked the world they lived in and the world they had brought their children into. World wars, starvation and class division were being defeated and they did not welcome their mother constantly dragging them back into that distant past. Her great age and uncomplicated mind, though, gave her a unique perspective. The generation above her had fought the Crimean War and she herself had lived through the Boer War, the First World War and the Second World War in quick succession; so why on earth should anybody believe there would be no more wars? The Germans had tried to take over the world twice in her lifetime, therefore to her it stood to reason that they would, sooner or later, try again. Why would anyone actually *buy* a house when somebody could fly over one day and drop a bomb on it? This is how she saw the world. Her world was completely coloured by her own experiences and her mind was pure and untainted by media messages and agendas, educational conditioning and intellectual or social strictures. This made her almost unique in the 1980s.

That other world occasionally came back to haunt them all. For the boys, they had left it behind purposely. For Nell, she had merely outlived it. It was nearly 40 years since her last surviving sibling, Bill, had died but every now and then something happened that would bring those days hurtling back and remind them all of how it once was and where they all came from. One Charlie Sunday, she had been happily reading her *Sunday Express* before Charlie Boy actually arrived when she turned to a two-page spread in a series reviving old murder cases. Staring at her and smirking knowingly from the page was Tichy Thorogood. There was, of course, no mention of Maggs or any connection to the Bradshaw family whatsoever, but she angrily screwed the paper into a ball and burnt it in the grate. When Charlie arrived, she told him she felt unwell and was going to have to go back to bed, such was the effect of Tichy's uninvited and unexpected presence in her home.

Another time, Ted arrived at Nell's and he was clearly distressed. His own son was now taking his O levels at school and had chosen his family history as his project for his history course. This involved Ted and his boy, Martin, visiting Nell more than was usual and gleaning what information they could to assist and flesh out their searching of more official channels. During these conversations, the name Harry Cousins would crop up and Nell and Ted would recall what a young rascal he was and wonder how life had panned out for him. Ted had heard nothing of him since 1949, when his importation business was said to be doing well. What he subsequently unearthed shook him to the core. Through a mutual friend rediscovered, Ted was told that Harry Cousins had stuck his head in a gas oven and had taken his own life in 1958. He was married with children and his business was extremely successful. He had homes in London and Italy and enjoyed a good lifestyle. The line at the time of his death was that his suicide was totally inexplicable, as Harry Cousins was the man who had everything. Yet the mutual friend confided in Ted the sort of detail that is often missing when news of a suicide is relayed.

Harry had needed to renew or reapply for a passport or visa and this required obtaining a copy of his birth certificate from Somerset House. This he did and he studied it for the first time. He was mortified to read that his mother and father were not his mother and father, as he had understandably believed all of his life, but were in fact his older brother and sister with whom he had lived in the cramped cottage in Fulham. His parents, then, were actually his grandparents. These revelations had devastated him. The house in which Harry had committed suicide belonged to his sister-mother.

Although it had been nearly 40 years since Ted and Harry Cousins had had any contact, the revelation hit him hard and he went to his mother to share the news and try to make sense of it.

'Poor little imp,' said Nell, shaking her head.

Ted recalled the house near the Chelsea football ground in the little square and all those children, hollow-cheeked and sunken-eyed, and could only now start to imagine the lives that were being lived out between those four damp walls.

''Ow could something like that 'appen?' he asked of his mother.

'It 'appened a lot in them days. 'Specially when I was a nipper. Nobody talked about it, that's all.'

Ted looked at his mother's pained expression and realised for the first time there was so, so much she kept to herself.

XXIII

The End of the Century

'Mr Knight? Mr Harry Knight?'

'Yes, Harry Knight speaking.'

'Good morning, Mr Knight. I am Mrs Redcliffe from The Oaks. We met a couple of days ago at your mother's 100th birthday party.'

Harry thought he knew what was coming.

'Well, I have some mixed news for you. Your mother is speaking again and she has become remarkably lucid, but she has told us she has decided to die and is refusing to take any food. In fact, she told us this the day after the party. Her mind seems to have come back, but she is fading away physically, I'm afraid. The doctor has asked me to seek your permission to feed her intravenously and says we may need to send her to St John's shortly.'

'We'll come and see you tomorrow morning, if that's all right with you, Mrs Redcliffe?'

Harry rang Ted and Ted rang Charlie Boy, and they arranged

to meet at the nursing home the following morning.

In a pleasant bedroom in Putney on a rainy morning in 1988 sat four people connected by blood and Battersea, although none of them lived there now. Charlie and Harry held one of Nell's hands each on either side of the bed and Ted pulled a stool up close to his mother's ear.

'Mum, we're all here. Charlie, Harry and Ted.'

There was no response, but the old lady's chest rose and fell healthily. The room was quiet, the only sounds being the old lady's breathing and the muffled dialogue from a television in the next room. The three men started to talk about old times. Capturing and savouring what they knew would be the last occasion all four of them would be together in this life. They spoke to Nell, although she appeared to be in a deep sleep, and they spoke to each other. All sorts of emotions bubbled and rippled between them. Talk of weddings, parties, day trips and holidays; uncles, aunties, cousins and friends; incidents and accidents. Although tears were lurking behind eyes, they were laughing and chuckling together as they bathed in their family bonds and familiarity.

'Do you remember when we went to see *Oh, Mr Porter!* at the Pavilion? You were home on leave, I think, Harry. How embarrassing. She talked aloud all the way through it. Kept answering old Will Hay back,' remembered Ted.

They laughed and shook their heads at the memory. 'I wouldn't go into a cinema with her,' said Harry, 'not after the commissionaire threatened to chuck her out for laughing all through *King Kong*. She thought it was a comedy.'

'What year would that have been?' enquired Charlie.

'You'd have been a baby, Charlie Boy,' Harry answered. 'It was 1934, I think.'

'Later than that. I can remember going to see it with my pals, old Fay Wray and Bruce Cabot. Never forget it,' Ted argued.

'1937.' Her eyes were still closed, but the words were clear enough and the voice strong.

'Mum, you can hear us. You can speak.'

A tiny smile flickered across her mouth, revealing only gums. Her eyelids rolled upwards with great effort and threatened to roll back for a second but watery, yellowed eyes revealed themselves. '*Oh, Mr Porter!* was 1937,' she expanded.

'How are you feeling, Mum?'

'Gawd take me,' she moaned. She had been saying this since she was 90, an age she had judged it was indecent to live beyond, but the months and years rolled on without any disease claiming her.

'Gawd is not taking you anywhere, Mum. You're as fit as a fiddle. You're an old warhorse. There's ten years in you, Mum. You'll outlive me and 'Arry, you will,' Ted said firmly. He knew it was not true.

'It's time for me to go.'

She turned her head to her right and looked straight at Harry. Her eyes searched his. She could see her husband, Henry, in his kind features and he could see that determination in his mother's eyes he knew so well. It was a determination that got her and most of the people of her generation through the most difficult of times. They were made of such stoical stuff, Harry reflected.

'I know, Mum.' Harry leant forward and kissed the most remarkable woman he ever knew on the forehead. Charlie could not stop the tears filling up in his eyes and Ted pressed his mother's hand against his cheek. The moment held. Nobody wanted to let it go. Four people locked in a human chain of love, peace and the past.

Mrs Redcliffe waited outside the room and as the three sombre, almost elderly men emerged, she looked to Harry Knight for some guidance.

'We don't want you to feed her intravenously, Mrs Redcliffe.'

'That could pose some ethical difficulties for us.'

'Don't worry. If my mother has decided to die, she will get there very quickly.'

The three men walked outside, where three separate cars were parked.

'Who fancies a pint down the Mason's Arms? It's only up the road,' Ted suggested.

'We know where it is.'

And off they went in separate cars, each absorbing different but similar memories as they passed through Wandsworth into the Battersea of their childhood and youth. A place that on the surface was recognisable only in patches but that still stirred them all in ways they did not fully comprehend. The Mason's was a pub all three of them had used as young men. In their day, it was popular with the chaps of Battersea before they started their courting. As they entered, they were pleased to note that, despite changes in the decor, the layout of the pub had changed very little. There were six or seven customers dotted around the bar, mainly middle-aged and elderly men with tobacco tins and newspapers opened up on the racing pages. They spoke among themselves and were obviously familiar with each other but all sat separately.

'Do you remember sitting in here and listening to the blind kid playing the piano?' Harry asked of his companions.

Ted could. 'Course I do. George Shearing was 'is name. 'Is mum used to bring him in that door there and lead him over to the piano there, where the jukebox is now. 'E was a great little pianist. 'E's a massive star now out in America. Didn't know that, did you?'

'Really? Mum used to say that he had done well and made records with Frank Sinatra and Dean Martin, but I just put it down to her imagination.'

'No, it's all true. The family lived just over the back here. So at least one Battersea boy made it good.'

'You haven't done so bad,' Harry said, patting his brother's shoulder as he passed him a pint.

'And you ain't done so bad either, 'Arry. And you, Charlie Boy. We've all done OK, considering.'

They settled down with their drinks, wondering how well they had done and how many of Nell's fantastic stories and beliefs were rooted in truth.

'You know she thought Max Miller was Tichy Thorogood or Tichy's son,' laughed Ted.

'I remember that.'

'Who exactly is this Tichy Thorogood?' interjected Charlie Boy.

The brothers realised for the first time that Charlie must never have been told. He had no idea. It had all happened before he was born and Tichy was clearly not talked about by the family when he was young. By the time he was old enough to be told, there had been no immediate family left to tell him. After 1940, things had moved so fast. It made them realise how little time they had spent together as adults in these last 40 years; how adult life and a world that gathers speed each day robs everyone of basic conversation and the ability to really know each other and nourish family relationships. Ted looked to his older brother for a steer. Harry shrugged and the next half-hour was filled with the story of Maggs, Tichy and the tragic young country policeman.

Charlie was agog as a whole chapter of his mother's life was revealed to him. His mum and a murderer? The legend of Bonnie and Clyde flashed into his mind. Charlie had read about the murder in true-crime books and he could not believe he and his family were in a small way connected to it. He also could not believe that Nell had never let anything slip. Discretion was never her strong point.

'You know, she would very rarely talk about my mum and dad. Sometimes I felt she did not like them,' volunteered Charlie, the revelations about his mother and Tichy having opened up his emotions.

'Not at all, Charlie. She loved Maggs like mad. She was her little sister. That's why she socked old Tichy on the jaw, because he disrespected her. She just buried these things deep. She never talks about the girls, does she? Your poor sisters. Too painful.' Harry stopped and looked into his pint, not wishing to stir up Charlie's feelings about his sisters.

'You're right, Harry, I'm sure, but I don't think she ever forgave my dad for killing himself. She didn't approve of suicide, did she? I remember when that boxer Freddie Mills killed himself. Anyone would have thought he'd gone out on a murder spree, the way she carried on.'

'It was a big shock, Charlie Boy. In those days, it was different. She thought it was a sin, but she loved your old dad. 'E was a good man and she knew it,' said Ted.

'Was he? I can't really remember him,' Charlie sighed. 'Mum rarely spoke of him and when she did, it was not with any real affection, know what I mean? Nobody actually said anything, but there was this feeling that he'd done something wrong. That he was bad. They weren't no photos up of him.'

'Like I say, Charlie, things was different then. Suicide was something that got swept under the carpet. If you 'ad one, that is. 'Arry'll tell you, your dad was a diamond. A lovely man. 'E was like a father to me and 'Arry and took us out all over the place. 'E was like a big kid 'imself. We used to get 'im climbing the trees up Box Hill for birds' eggs. 'E taught me to swim in the pond up on Clapham Common. I suppose when the shops went bad 'e just couldn't see an end to it. I reckon 'e must 'ave thought that you'd all be better off without 'im. Things were so bad then, you can see 'ow people got like that.'

Harry could see Charlie sinking into his seat and noticed he was blinking back tears and twitching more vigorously. This was probably the first time he had ever discussed his father with anyone that actually knew him.

'Charlie, he was always cheerful, though. With us. And your mum loved him, I'm sure of that. And he adored her. He was full of jokes. That's how I remember him. Don't you remember him at all?'

Charlie pondered a little, 'I just have this memory of sitting on his lap and him blowing on a mouth organ.' He smiled at the memory.

Ted went to his jacket pocket, now draped over the arm of his chair. 'What, this one?' He outstretched his palm to reveal Charlie Melchior's old harmonica complete with thin tartan ribbon.

'It's not! It's not!'

'It is.' Ted laid it on the table in front of his cousin. ''E came round and gave it to me the night before he died.'

Charlie, utterly awestruck, picked it up and gently ran his finger along it before gripping it tightly in his fist – the harmonica connecting him to his father more solidly than anything else ever had.

'He's played this. My dad played this. It's been in his mouth. I can't believe it.'

'He played it all the flippin' time,' Harry chuckled.

Ted reached and took the mouth organ from Charlie and blew into it a couple of times, tapped it on the table and launched into 'Danny Boy'. It was beautiful. There were a few more drinkers in the bar by now and stools squeaked as they were turned to face the table where the three old men sat. Conversations were halted. Smiles lit up red faces. The tune and the instrument stimulating buried memories in several different minds. When Ted was finished, there was a small but heartfelt ripple of applause. All three men wiped a tear or two from their eyes, and Ted wiped the harmonica on his sleeve and handed it over to Charlie.

'Keep it.'

Another round of drinks was ordered and more stories recalled and the mood lightened again.

'I remember when we had a speech day at Salesian's,' Harry recalled. 'I was dreading her coming. Most of the kids' parents were better off and much younger than Mum. You know how it is when you're a boy – these things matter. All the parents were arriving through the main gates, some in cars, and I spot her – she's taken a short cut and has come through a gap in the fence and is marching across the school field. She had that blasted hat on, the one with the ridiculous feather, and her black trench coat and a brooch like a bloody iron cross hanging off it. She was swinging her arms like she was arriving for a prize fight. I wanted the ground to open up and swallow me. When I went up to get my prize, she gave me a standing ovation – all the other mums and dads had just sat and clapped politely. I knew she would.'

'She was a character.'

'A real character. They won't make any more like her. She was made of stronger stuff than us.'

'She certainly was.'

All three men allowed the conversation to drop off as they considered Nell's character and her life.

Finally, Ted drained his glass and asked disingenuously, 'Why are we talking about her in the past tense? She could surprise us all yet.'

They drank two more pints each that lunchtime, far more than they were accustomed to in recent years, and toasted the memory of Nell and their own past before they scooped up their keys and headed back outside to their cars, knowing that by the time they arrived back to their respective houses they would hear the news of Nell Tregent's passing.

WANDSWORTH NEWS

27 March 1988

TREGENT, ELLEN, previously Knight, née Bradshaw, of Battersea. Born 1888. Passed peacefully away in her sleep on 19 March 1988 aged 100 years. Shall be greatly missed by her boys, Harry, Ted and Charlie, and her grandchildren and great-grandchildren.

She was a mother to so many.

The funeral has already taken place.